ENGLISH WATER-COLOURS

Frontispiece

J. M. W. TURNER (1775–1851)

May Chickens or *The Cottage Steps*
By courtesy of the Leger Galleries

ENGLISH WATER-COLOURS

Stanley W. Fisher

WARD LOCK LIMITED
LONDON

SBN 7063 1888 9

Ward Lock Limited, 116 Baker Street, London W1M 2BB

Printed in Great Britain by Richard Clay (The Chaucer Press), Ltd., Bungay, Suffolk

DEDICATION

To Albert and Daisy Hollis

AUTHOR'S NOTE

As a lover, collector and former teacher of water-colour painting it is my hope that this book may perhaps make a few converts among those who undervalue it as compared with painting in oils. It is neither an inferior art nor an easier one—mistakes cannot be covered up, and spontaneity is essential to success. The book is intended to be an introduction only, and its size precludes any attempt to be comprehensive. I have tried, however, to mention artists whose work may be considered as representative of the many ways in which the medium has been used, whose drawings have in some way or another advanced development or whose names are well known to the average collector. At the same time I have included the names of lesser known men, and in some cases illustrated their work, because I feel that in fact it is a common error to attribute their drawings to those who for some reason are better known. Value in the visual arts is too often measured by reputation rather than by merit.

So far as illustrations are concerned, I have tried to avoid the inclusion of too many drawings which, being in well-known collections, have been repeatedly reproduced in so many books, however excellent they may be. At the same time I have done my best by careful examination and research to ensure that all are authentic and typical. I have not always been able

to find signed examples—and it must be acknow-
ledged that not all signatures are genuine—and inevitably perhaps some of my attributions may be
disputed, particularly since an illustration leaves so
much to the imagination, and gives so much less information than did the original. My thanks are due to
the Victoria and Albert Museum, British Museum,
Leger Gallery and to collector friends who have so
kindly provided me with excellent photographs.

Stanley W. Fisher

CONTENTS

PART I

1

THE BEGINNINGS OF
WATER-COLOUR PAINTING

JUSTLY proud though the collector may be of the excellence of British water-colour painting from the late eighteenth century onwards, it must be accepted that its beginnings were alien, since the methods of sixteenth-and seventeenth-century Dutch and German artists were adapted and developed into a British style quite unlike anything which had gone before.

Up to the fourteenth century the monks who illustrated manuscripts did in fact paint in transparent water-colour, until such time as it was found that body-colour or gouache, with the colours mixed with Chinese white, gave an opaque, more solid appearance which produced a more lasting and effective foundation for their gold embellishment. The next stage was provided by miniature painters, who worked first on vellum applied to the backs of playing cards and later, after about 1685, on ivory. Edward Norgate, writing early in the seventeenth century, rightly claimed the superiority of water-colour over oil painting for this delicate purpose, and at the same time tells us, perhaps surprisingly, that landscapes as well as miniatures were painted on vellum, with much use of body-colour. All this, of course, took place a

ANGELICA KAUFFMANN (1741–1807)

Angelica and Medro

long time before water-colours were painted in this country.

It is known that first in a long line of artists who were inspired by European scenery of the grander kind, and apart from such masters as Sir Anthony Van Dyck (1599–1641) and Peter Paul Rubens (1577–1640) who made their rough sketches in water-colour, was the great Albrecht Dürer (1471–1528). He worked in water-colour in the Alps (on a 1490 journey), in Nüremberg and, in 1520–21, in the Netherlands, drawing with a pen and washing over with pure water-colour, with an occasional use of body-colour. It is interesting to know that at such an early date he was familiar with a principle that was so much later to be re-introduced by Cotman and others, of shading a colour with a darker tone of the same colour.

During the seventeenth century there was an important school of water-colour painting in Holland, taking the form of colour-washed drawings in chalk or ink, and practised by such men as Adrian Van Ostade (1610–71), Albert Cuyp (1620–91) and Hans Bol (1534–93). Little attempt was made at actual faithfulness of colour or indeed at exact application, since the intent was merely to add liveliness and warmth, and this limited colour was seldom used in the large washes which became a noted characteristic of the English school. It was not intended to be essential to the drawing, but rather to give it depth.

The miniaturists or 'portrait limners' working in sixteenth- and seventeenth-century England and on the Continent occasionally placed their subjects before a landscape or architectural background, thereby becoming the unconscious initiators of the school of later topographical painters. One of the earliest of these was John White, who accompanied Sir Walter Raleigh (1552–1618) on his Virginia expedition, was later made Governor of the colony and made water-colour drawings of its scenery, its natives and its customs, some of which were made into engravings for Theodore de Bry's 'America'. At the same time a very different kind of water-colour drawing, though equally suited to the delicacy of the medium, was being practised by Jacques Le Moyne de Morgues, who died in 1588. His subjects were English plants, flowers and fruits, though he was a Frenchman who escaped the St. Bartholomew massacre to be employed, also by Raleigh, in London. As was so often the case in the early days, the drawings were intended to be made into engravings, and show microscopically exact drawing coupled with pure colour, occasionally reinforced with body-colour.

Inigo Jones (1573–1652) is best known for his skill as an architect, but he was associated with Ben Jonson in the production of masques, for which he designed costumes and scenery. His sketches, many of which may be seen at Chatsworth, were mostly drawn in ink and washed in sepia, though a few were done in pure colour applied with a full brush. What, above all, is extremely interesting is that although at this time landscape was generally alien to British art, there is evidence to show that Jones was indeed a landscape painter, his work referred to by Vertue (Vertue—I, 'Autobiography', *Walpole Society*, XVIII, 1929–30, p. 148) as 'innumerable fine Views' in 'beautifull (*sic*) Variety', a reference which is logically supported by the presumption that he drew such scenery as the 'landscape consisting of small woods' referred to by Ben Jonson in stage directions for a masque in 1605. It would also appear that seascape painting (or 'sea-schap') began at much the same

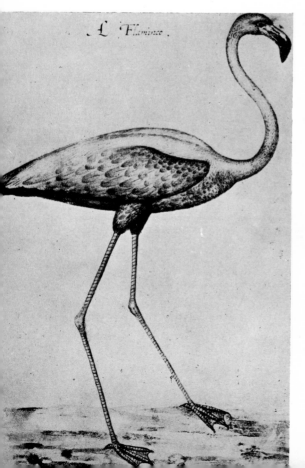

JOHN WHITE
(1577–1590)
A Flamingo

15

time, as was logical, and Vertue refers to Samuel Scott (*c.* 1702–72), in 1732, as a 'sea-schap painter'.

There must have been many roads by which landscape painting travelled from the Continent to this country, and we have space to suggest but a few of them. Peter Paul Rubens came over to the Court of Charles I in 1629, and he had then been a watercolourist for some twenty years, drawing usually with a pen, and washing in with pale, transparent colour or with body-colour. His work was greatly admired by the King, and it follows that it would attract wide attention. He was followed to London by Van Dyck in 1632, examples of whose work in water-colour are to be seen in many collections, including those of J. Pierpoint Morgan and Sir W. Fitzherbert. A notable feature of this master's work, having regard to its early date, is the emphasis on colour shape, on mass, and an absence of the outline which is such a distinct feature of the 'tinted drawing' style of the early topographers. As Martin Hardie has pointed out, he worked much in the style of Thomas Gainsborough (1727–88).

In contrast to such almost modern use of colour mass, we may next consider the quite different but equally notable early topographical work of Wenceslaus Hollar (1607–77), born at Prague and brought to England in 1636 as the protégé of Thomas Howard, Earl of Arundel, to spend the rest of his life in this country. He was the originator of the Dutch tinted drawing, in which pen sketches were washed in lightly with water-colour which, in his case at any

SIR JAMES THORNHILL (1675–1734)
River at Hampton Court

rate, was limited to blue, yellow, green, brown and rose madder. Twenty of his drawings are at Chatsworth, made as a record (just as we would use a camera) of the Earl's stay as ambassador to the Court of Ferdinand II in 1636, and others were done in Morocco, where he was sent by the Government in 1669. Most interesting to us, perhaps, are his many representations of the buildings of seventeenth-century London, a considerable number of which were engraved. His style is indeed more often that of an engraver, with much use of parallel lines, for it must be remembered that Hollar was first and foremost an accurate recorder, though on occasion, and as exemplified in his etchings of Surrey scenery, he had a keen eye for what was later to be called the 'picturesque'.

Francis Place (1647–1728) was a follower of Hollar, with whom he was friendly, and his sketch-books and drawings indicate that he travelled widely through England, Wales and Ireland. Whereas Hollar was obliged to work on a pittance, however, Place was apparently independent, and so less inclined towards accurate representation—he was able to indulge his fancy. He therefore followed the looser style occasionally used by Hollar, drawing his views with a pen and adding sepia or indian ink shadows (not washed over with colour as in later years) and mere touches of colour.

Among the first English artists to adopt the tinted drawing style was Francis Barlow, (*c.* 1626–1702). He was a portrait painter, but his genius lay in animal, bird and fish painting, often with landscape backgrounds, some of which were made into etchings by Francis Place. Another Barlow, Edward, born in 1642, was 'discovered' in 1934, when the illustrated manuscript of his *Journal* was exhibited for the first time. He became a seaman, and in a simple but detailed manner illustrated the record of his travels with drawings of storms, shipping, coastal landscapes, birds, beasts and fishes. These were drawn with a fine pen in a brownish ink, his colours bright in viridian green, blue, yellow, yellow ochre, brown, vermilion and rose madder, very much the same colours in fact as were used by contemporary map-makers.

From such sources as these, of such varied character, was derived water-colour as a medium for picture-making. Its advent was in fact most opportune, since it coincided with a social and incidentally aesthetic desire by English gentlemen to travel abroad and to bring back a pictorial record of their travels. For this purpose the simple, quick and readily transportable medium was ideal, while the results could be easily kept in portfolios, to be later studied in comfort. It was a custom which began as a social one, but which inevitably led to a better appreciation of landscape, and so to a search for suitable subjects. Some wealthy travellers took their artists with them, while others, who preferred to make their own drawings, gave a livelihood to professional drawing-masters, whose styles, circulated by the drawings they made to be copied by their pupils, have become familiar to present-day students of the art.

AUGUSTUS CHARLES PUGIN (1764–1832)

The High Street, Oxford

20

2

THE TECHNIQUES OF
WATER-COLOUR PAINTING

WATER-COLOUR painting is a method by which the pigments used are transferred to the sheet of paper or other substance on which the painting is done by mixing them with water. The water evaporates, leaving a stain on the paper. This is, of course, an elementary definition which needs amplification. In the first place, unless some kind of fixing medium is added to the water or to the pigment itself, the colour will not adhere, and many substances have been used for the purpose, usually added to the pigment, and including gum arabic, flour or rice paste, and egg yolk and white. As we have seen in the previous chapter, much water-colour drawing was done in ink, which again would not adhere without the presence of a fixing agent.

Nowadays whatever gum or other fixative is needed is added by the makers of the colour, whether in cake or tube form, and the artist need add only water. Then, since the essence of a water-colour is translucency, the aim is to avoid overmuch working upon the surface of the paper by applying the colour in clean, clear washes, the purest effect being obtained by using a large, dripping brush for everything apart from detail. The brilliancy thus achieved arises from the fact that transparent water-colour will always reveal more or less of the white paper upon which it is painted, giving an effect of light that is, of course, less when darker tints are used. The work of an unskilled beginner is often betrayed by muddy shadows and a dry, dragged appearance, the result of working with too dry a brush.

Much experiment has been made to produce satisfactory paper, and we cannot here discuss the many varieties, whether hand or (later) machine made, white or tinted, rough, granulated or smooth, which have been preferred by artists as being best suited to their styles. Early papers used during the seventeenth and eighteenth centuries were of the kind known as 'laid', of fine quality and colour, but extremely thin and fragile, made to limited size and folded into quires so that large drawings often show a pronounced crease. During the second half of the eighteenth century paper-makers, knowing that the little hillocks and hollows in a granulated paper helped the water-colourist to achieve added luminosity, and that many were wont to scrape or scrub their dried drawings, produced such improved papers as those made by Whatman and the 'Creswick' papers of which Peter De Wint was especially fond. Many artists found their own papers, suited to their own particular technique, as did David Cox when he accidentally found in 1836 a Scottish wrapping paper on which so much of his later work was done. In the early part of the century it was common to stain paper to give warmer tints, with bistre, with water coloured with tobacco leaves and even with beer. And, of course, water-colourists have always been wont to paint upon a surface previously stained with a thin wash of colour. Every water-colourist has his own preference, rough or smooth, thin or thick, according to his own particular technique.

As opposed to pure water-colour, as has already been mentioned, we have body-colour or gouache, in which the colours have been mixed with Chinese white to give opacity. Some pigments, such as vermilion and cobalt blue, are already semi-opaque. While it has always been common practice to use touches of body-colour for highlights, as an alternative, for instance, to scraping away ripples in water, breaking wave-tops or tree-trunk details, we find many drawings painted entirely in the medium, though its use has always been much criticised by the lover of pure water-colour, since no use whatever is made of the whiteness of the paper. Nevertheless, notable exponents of body-colour, in one way or another, include Paul Sandby, Turner, De Wint, J. F. Lewis, Birket Foster, Louis Haghe, William Henry Hunt and Samuel Palmer.

Every artist of note had his own particular range of pigment—a knowledge of which is often an aid to attribution—and many in their writings have given their own opinions of what colours should be used, often advising, as did Edward Dayes, that the water-colourist should make his own. In 1809, in his *Drawing in Watercolours*, James Roberts gave a list of twelve essential colours, excluding black. It is on record that as early as 1675 Sir Godfrey Kneller employed a man solely to make his colours, though it is doubtful whether the artist's colourman was in general existence before about 1750. Matthew Darly advertised 'transparent colours for staining drawings' in 1776, and an early mention of Reeves is by a writer in 1811, some ten years before he introduced pigments in the form of small soluble cakes. His invention was followed by others, until about 1830–40

ALEXANDER COZENS (*c.* 1717–86)

A Castle in a Landscape

Winsor and Newton offered colours made up in pans, or fitting directly into the divisions in japanned boxes, treated with honey or glycerine so as to remain moist. Finally, about 1847 the same firm put moist colours into metal tubes. It is, of course, a mistake to imagine that every possible colour can be made by mixing the primary colours, and from time to time water-colourists have invented pigments for their own use which have ever since been produced commercially—a typical example is the useful 'Payne's Grey', invented by William Payne.

The usual practice in making a water-colour drawing has always been to make a preliminary drawing with pencil, charcoal, chalk or ink, either in the form of a complete work in itself or merely consisting of a few indications of the outstanding features of the composition. Many artists, including Alexander Cozens and Paul Sandby, made their own ink, whether black or sepia, and a common practice was to add additional touches to finished colour treatment. Turner did this, as did Samuel Prout when he added his well-known 'broken line' to an architectural drawing. Some artists preferred to emphasise outline with a fine brush. An important aid to attribution is indeed very often the manner in which the initial drawing or later touching-up is done.

Brushes (or 'pencils' as they were once called) first had quill handles until about 1850, and though such are still made, the wooden handle is usual nowadays. The water-colourist uses brushes made of red sable or camel's hair, though some still use large wash brushes made of hog's hair. There is much to be said for using brushes as large as possible for the purpose in hand, though we do not nowadays use such large ones as were preferred by the early water-colourists. The hairs—even of a large brush—should always come to a point; such was the advice given by James Roberts in 1809 (*Painting in Water-colour*), and at the same time he recommended very small camel's hair brushes for very small figures or for the rigging of vessels.

The first requirement of a water-colour painter is the ability to lay an even wash, swiftly, always with a full brush, ('The pencil should be full of colour in order that it may float,' says David Cox), working from left to right, from top to bottom, preferably with the paper slightly sloping so that the colour runs down. W. Hall, in his *Biography of David Cox*, tells how he has seen 'the colour running down his paper in streams.' As skill develops an artist is able to graduate his work from dark to light, and vice-versa. The early topographers used a single thin wash, but later artists placed wash upon wash, allowing parts of the under washes to show through. It is clear that different effects, notably in the treatment of skies, are obtained by applying such later washes over a wet, damp or dry surface at will; Thomas Girtin and Peter De Wint worked in this way, and because a dry paper gives hard edges, some water-colourists preferred to work on a paper previously dampened by a wash of water. Another kind of wash, the 'dragged' or broken wash, is applied from a dampened brush charged with almost dry colour, which takes advantage of a rough paper by leaving tiny, lighter points to show to good effect, for example, in the treatment of brickwork or stone. An entirely different method of painting is by means of 'stippling', when the pigment is applied in the form of dots with the point of the brush, in the manner of Birket Foster and William Henry Hunt, not to be confused with the effect obtained by means of separate touches or strokes of a wet brush which is often seen in the work of David Cox.

Colour having been applied, it cannot be lightened by adding a lighter colour, and the only resource is to use body-colour, to lift off some of the colour, or even to remove it entirely to show the paper beneath, which can then be repainted if necessary. There are several ways of doing this. The pigment may be wetted with the brush and removed with a rag, india-rubber or blotting-paper, as Girtin used to do—W. H. Pyne recommended the use of dry bread, a method employed to good effect by John Sell Cotman. Francis Nicholson invented a way of painting light foliage and highlights against a dark background, though he made little use of it himself; briefly, the parts intended to be lighter were first painted in with a composition of turpentine, bees-wax and flake-white, which when washed over with the darker colour resisted it, and was removed with turpentine when the drawing was dry. So far as shadows are concerned, the early method was to paint them in with, for example, Prussian blue and brown ink (according to Edward Dayes) or, later, as Girtin and Turner began to do, to wash in objects in colour and then shadow with darker tones of the same colour.

When a drawing is dry its appearance may be altered or improved in many ways. Though water-colour is then surprisingly resistant to water, dark or overpainted portions can be lightened or softened by scrubbing under a tap, or colour may be removed with the point of a knife to show the paper beneath in the shape of ripples on water and other highlights, after which the roughened surface may be smoothed with a hard, rounded point. A very early process, used by J. S. Cotman, James Holland and Turner, was to lift highlights by removing the wet paint with the wooden end of a brush, leaving quite a hard, dark edge, whereas if a brush or rag and water had been used the result would have been a soft edge. Most incongruous of all the many finishing touches, perhaps, was the attempt by some early water-colourists to imitate the appearance of oil-paintings by varnishing their finished work, a practice recommended by Francis Nicholson, though he himself seldom made use of it. Alternatively, others, such as John Varley and Henry Edridge, used gum arabic to give depth to darker parts of their work, the use of which is betrayed by an unattractive gloss when the light falls at an angle across the drawing.

3

THE EIGHTEENTH-CENTURY WATER-COLOURISTS

THE earliest English water-colours which can be considered to be typical of the period are the 'tinted drawings' of the second half of the eighteenth century, drawn in ink, shadowed in grey and washed in with colour. The professional artist worked predominantly for the engraver—so that his colour was in the nature of an embellishment and not essential— and private buyers of drawings for art's sake were very few. Thus, the names of many who drew for books of engraved views are forgotten, and we cannot wonder that many early water-colourists, knowing how little their efforts were to be valued for their own sake, did not think of signing them.

The gradual change from this state of affairs was due to several reasons. In the first place, as has already been suggested, the eyes of the wealthy were opened to the beauties of foreign landscape, and the cult of the 'picturesque' became fashionable, while at the same time the acquisition of drawings of their houses and estates was much simplified by the new art, in contrast to the expense incurred by the paraphernalia, smelly and cumbersome, of the painter of portraits in oils. An equally important factor in the growing popularity of water-colour drawing was also a social one, when the wealthy dilettante with time on his hands welcomed its cleanliness, and was able to pass the time pleasurably when 'taking the waters'. Gainsborough lived at Bath, the mecca not only of the invalid but also of the fashionable, and his presence doubtless soon attracted a host of amateurs as well as a considerable body of drawing-masters. His work, however, was quite outside the use of water-colour proper, and had little influence on the art.

Among these drawing-masters was Alexander Cozens (1710–86), who with his son John (1752–*c.* 1797) had enormous influence on the development of water-colour. He published *A New Method of Drawing Original Landscapes*, virtually a short-cut system for the amateur, which earned for him the self-explanatory title of 'Blotmaker General to the Town', though he himself worked mainly in monochrome, while his son, painting in the 'tinted drawing' style, earned the admiration of John Constable and Turner by his mastery of atmosphere and his vigorous penwork, tinted with indigo, yellow ochre, india-red, burnt umber and burnt sienna.

John Cozens was one of the first water-colourists who drew much inspiration from Italy—which he visited first in 1776—and among others who followed his example and were similarly affected were Francis Towne (*c.* 1740–1816) and his teacher and friend

William Pars (1742–82). Towne's style is individual, marked by neat though fluent outlining in pen, and a great understanding of the value of large, clear areas of pure colour which yet, as in some of his Welsh drawings of about 1777–80, impart the indescribably grand, almost austere effect which is so characteristic of his work. His best drawings were done in the Italian Alps, where he was able to render in this style, often in brilliant colour, the diagonals and triangles of the towering rock faces that we see in such works as 'The Source of the Arveiron with the Part of Mont Blanc', which is in the Victoria and Albert Museum.

It was as a draughtsman that William Pars was chosen to accompany a party of artists and architects to Greece in 1764, and on other occasions he went to Italy, Switzerland (with Lord Palmerston) and Ireland. His short life means that comparatively few of his drawings are to be seen, many of them badly faded, but at best they show a full range of brilliant colour, sometimes deepened with gum in the brownish shadows. On the whole, his English and Irish subjects are low-toned, in soft greys, greens and browns. Though he is known as a landscape painter, he himself loved drawing figures, large groups of which he introduced into architectural drawings, precisely and delicately drawn.

Another early water-colourist of this period who travelled extensively was William Marlow (1740–1813), a pupil of Samuel Scott, who first exhibited with the Society of Artists in 1762. At this time he

was known as a proficient painter of country man-
sions, but his sense of the picturesque was broadened
by a visit abroad to France and Italy in 1765. After
his return in 1768 most of his best work was done in
the Thames Valley—he died in Twickenham—and
his views of London, such as 'Fish Street Hill and the
Monument' (British Museum) are strongly effective.
Marlow was a true craftsman, working in oils and in
every kind of water-colour, using strong, sometimes
heavy and raw colour, which leads many to prefer
his monochromes, beautifully drawn in ink. He had a
trick of placing small figures at strategic points in his
compositions, coloured brightly in effective contrast
to the greens, greys and blues of a landscape.

The names of Paul Sandby (*c.* 1725–1809) and his
brother Thomas (*c.* 1721–98) are familiar to every
collector as outstanding exponents of the 'tinted
drawing', though on occasion Paul worked in gouache
which features a characteristic colour range of pearly
grey, rich blue-green and red. Both brothers had
long connections with Windsor Castle (Thomas lived
in the Park and was responsible for its lay-out), and
Paul's fame in particular has doubtless been greatly
enhanced by the Windsor Castle collection of his
drawings (*Sandby Drawings at Windsor Castle*, by
A. P. Oppé). Such reputation, however well deserved,
has two sides, for there can be little doubt that many
fine drawings credited to him were in fact painted by
lesser known but equally competent men. Jacob P.
Hackert (1737–1807), for instance, at his best was as
good a painter of trees, using a sparing pencil outline,

FRANCIS TOWNE (*c.* 1739–1816)

Grotto at Posilippo, Naples

THOMAS HEARNE
(1744–1817)

Wooded Glen at Downton, Hereford

a pleasing palette of greys, blues and greens, with grey shadows, and judiciously placed, Sandby-like, accurately drawn figures. Some Sandby work was influenced by the work of John Baptist Claude Chatelain (1710–71), formal and precise, drawn with a pen and palely washed. Indeed, there is a very long list of contemporary water-colourists who drew inspiration from the earliest topographers, from which we have space to select but a few. Anthony Devis (1729–1817), like Hackert, was fond of yellowish greens, blues and soft greys, and his trees often resemble those done by Marlow, but with characteristic foliage drawn with a series of loops, like bunches of bananas, parts of which, in his many sketches, he left in pencil, uncoloured. A typical English topographer of the same school was Samuel Hieronymous Grimm (1733–94), a Swiss settled in

England, and, above all, as is shown in his illustrations for Gilbert White's *Selborne*, the devoted recorder of rustic English landscape. Another Swiss, and friend of Grimm, was John Webber (*c.* 1750–93), who accompanied Captain Cook on his third and fatal voyage of 1776, and who is best known for his drawings of that voyage and for his Derbyshire views, washed in grey and brownish-grey over soft pencil, which he did in 1789. As opposed to those whose work was mainly topographical, we must not omit mention of their contemporaries whose leanings were towards architectural subjects, as for instance, Thomas Malton (1748–1804), famous for his lively, busy London views as shown in *A Picturesque Tour through the Cities of London and Westminster*, published in 1792, and his pupil Charles Wild (1781–1835), whose love was for the Gothic architecture of cathedrals abroad and in this country.

Among artists born during the first half of the century, Michael Angelo Rooker (1743–1801) demands mention, if only by reason of his highly finished and detailed technique, as seen in the topographical work done on a walking tour throughout England, some of it in monochrome, and other softly tinted over sparing outline in pencil or extremely fine pen. We have already said that many early water-colourists were also engravers, so closely linked were the two arts, and among those who were pupils of an engraver, in this case named William Woollett, were Benjamin Thomas Pouncy (d. 1799) and Thomas Hearne (1744–1817). Hearne was for three and a half years with Sir Ralph Payne, Governor General of the Leeward Islands, making drawings of the native life, but most of his work was done in this country, making illustrations for books of picturesque interest. Much of the best is in warm monochrome on coffee-tinted paper, and his coloured drawings, distinguished by accuracy of pencil or ink line, were carried out in delicate tones. His subjects generally centre around architectural interest, and he had a particularly tender way of depicting stone and brick-work. To the same generation belonged Joseph Farington (1747–1821), a master of delicate mono-chrome in sepia or blue-grey, washed in over pre-liminary faint outline and stronger black or brown ink. Little is known of Peter La Cave, a Frenchman who lived in England about 1794–1810; his pen-outlined wash drawings of gypsies, country girls and other rustic subjects are often confused with the somewhat similar work of Julius Caesar Ibbetson (1759–1817).

Amos Green (1735–1807), together with his artist wife Harriet Lister, formed an outstanding amateur team of Lake District water-colourists, painting in brown monochrome or in pale colour with soft green and yellow foliage and detailed bracken and other herbage in the foreground. Though earlier, his work is comparable with that of his namesake William Green (*c.* 1760–1823), who also painted in the Lake District, and whose work has an unmistakable brownish appearance, possibly due to the fading of the colours which he used.

Many of the finest though often lesser known

early water-colourists were amateurs. Coplestone Warre Bampfylde (1720–91) is a good example. He was a caricaturist but was also well known in his time as a landscapist, exhibiting freely between 1763 and 1783. He was clearly much influenced by Paul Sandby, especially in the imaginative compositions which he did extremely well. Gifted contemporary amateurs were the Rev. William Gilpin (1724–1804) and his brother Sawrey (1733–1807). Francis Grose (*c.* 1731–91) had a little training at a drawing school, which apparently did nothing to improve his generally poor technique, but he may serve very well as being outstandingly representative of the mid-eighteenth-century recorder of the picturesque antique for which he had a particularly good eye, and which he rendered in a pleasingly clear and fresh manner.

Earlier in this book we have seen how many wealthy men took with them on their travels, or even sent away to foreign parts, an artist who could make a pictorial record of foreign scenery. Such was John 'Warwick' Smith (1749–1831), pupil of Sawrey Gilpin, whose patron the Earl of Warwick supported him in Italy between 1776 and 1781. Above all, perhaps, Smith's ability to paint in so many different styles has made identification of his work difficult, for no class of it may be described as characteristic. On the other hand, Hugh William Williams (1773–1829) became so well known for his Grecian views, published between 1827 and 1829 in his *Select Views of Greece*, that he was nicknamed 'Grecian'. In fact, his Scottish drawings are the better known.

So far little mention has been made of seascape painting in water-colour, though it developed side by side with landscape. Nicholas Pocock (1740–1821), one of the original members of the 'Old Water-colour Society' (of which we shall have more to say later), was at once a topographer and a seascape painter. He in fact went to sea, and in 1767 commanded a vessel, the while he illustrated his journals with ink drawings, and when in port, as at Bristol, painted landscapes with shipping. His drawings in monochrome, often of groups of famous vessels, are sometimes superb, with meticulously penned rigging, and the general effect of his coloured drawings is one of blue and grey. Also a sailor, though a Gascon taken prisoner from a Spanish ship in 1758, was Dominic

JOHN CLEVELEY (1747–86)

View of the Old London Bridge, with Southwark Cathedral to the right

Serres (1722–93), who then stayed in England for the rest of his life, to become in 1768 a foundation member of the Royal Academy. His water-colours of shipping were drawn thickly in ink and tinted, as were those of Pocock, predominantly in blues and greys. His son, Dominic M. (1778–1804) was a drawing master, and the Victoria and Albert Museum has some of his decorative, rather dashing drawings, but his brother John Thomas (1759–1825) was the more accomplished, and in 1793 succeeded his father as marine painter to the King. Again, in his work we see the same pen drawing, in his case unhesitating and fluent, tinted in greys, blues and greens, often here and there relieved by touches of bright colour in, for example, seamen's clothes. John Cleveley, a

Deptford shipwright and himself a painter, had two sons, John (1747–86) and Robert (1747–1809), both of whom became seascape painters in water-colour. John was adept in the painting of choppy seas, and Robert was at his best in depicting naval battles. We should not forget the work of William Anderson (1757–1837), friend of Julius Caeser Ibbetson (1759–1817), whose drawings are accurate, often full of light and characteristically enlivened by the presence of figures in the foreground in red and blue jerseys or coats. Painting at the same time and in much the same manner was Samuel Atkins, whose dates of birth and death are not known, but who exhibited at the Royal Academy between 1787 and 1808.

Thomas Girtin (1775–1802) was short-lived, but he may be said to be well in the forefront of our greatest water-colourists, and such was his complete mastery of landscape, with his inimitable ability to depict wide acres of countryside in the small space of a piece of paper, that his work must be studied by the collector through the pages of such specialist books as *The Art of Thomas Girtin*, by Girtin and Loshak, and *Thomas Girtin*, by Jonothan Mayne. His rendering of architecture is superb, carried out in almost sombre colours of browns, greys and blue-greens. Although there is much pencil in his work, particularly in his buildings, when it is often extremely detailed, there is yet insufficient of it to make a picture if the colour were taken away; the exact opposite, of course, of a tinted drawing. Early tree treatment contains much fine linework, almost invisible, but in later years it was discarded. Girtin was much influenced by his teacher, Edward Dayes (1763–1804), a landscapist specialising in topographical subjects featuring architecture, for which he used a limited palette of brownish grey and blue enlivened with touches of brighter colours.

Philip de Loutherbourg (1740–1812) was a German who came to this country in 1771 to become Garrick's chief designer of scenery at Drury Lane, becoming an R.A. in 1781. His most characteristic water-colour work took the form of landscapes with cattle, usually in indian ink or sepia monochrome, but he also drew theatrical caricatures, illustrations for books, shipping and landscape. Another painter of scenery (at the King's Theatre and at Covent Garden) was Thomas Walmsley (1763–c. 1805), whose work is most indicative of his calling. Working always in body-colour, he painted dramatic, brooding landscapes in contrasting purple-browns and menacing orange-red. Like Loutherbourg, the German Franz Joseph Manskirsch (1770–1827) worked in England c. 1796–1805, painting mostly landscapes, often with figures in the style of George Morland.

There are some water-colourists who should be set apart from the main lines of development of the art at this early period. Francis Wheatley (1747–1801) is best known for his series of rather idealised 'Cries of London', and his work, sometimes insipid, is nevertheless invariably elegant and often, especially in his drawing of cattle, outstanding. A notable growth of interest in natural history in the middle of the century was responsible for the development of professional drawing in that sphere, as we see in the work, for example, of Thomas Bewick (1753–1828), author of many books and famous as a wood-engraver.

To this handful of representative eighteenth-century water-colourists, for it can be no more, we must add a few more names which cannot be omitted. Samuel Howitt (1765–1822) at first painted delightful tinted drawings of sporting and rustic subjects in the style of his brother-in-law Thomas Rowlandson, and later in life excelled in the drawing of animals, almost completely with the brush, upon a faint pencil outline. At a time when wealthy landowners were much preoccupied with prize livestock the much underrated J. Hornsey (*fl.* 1795–97) drew animals in watercolour. From the many teachers who were responsible for the success of so many great men we cannot perhaps do better than to mention Joseph Charles Barrow (*fl.* 1789–1802), almost unknown, underrated despite his rather wooden style and a watercolourist in the Sandby manner who taught John Varley.

4

THE NINETEENTH-CENTURY WATER-COLOURISTS

BY the beginning of the nineteenth century water-colour painting was recognised as an art in its own right but was still somewhat under a cloud, partly because the work of its devotees was apt to suffer when compared with paintings in oil-colours. True, some eminent water-colourists who also painted in oils, such as the Sandbys, Pars and M. A. Rooker, were original members of the Royal Academy, to be joined before 1800 by many others, but though exhibitions of water-colours had been held, and tentative efforts made to form societies, it was not until 1805 that one exclusively devoted to the promotion of water-colour was founded. At that time artists who painted only in that medium could not be elected to the Academy, their drawings when exhibited were, they claimed, poorly positioned, and in any case suffered when placed close to the stronger oil-paintings.

The prime mover in promoting the Society of Painters in Water Colours (usually known as the 'Old Society') was William Frederick Wells (1762–1836) and on 22nd April 1805, at 20 Lower Brook

Street, Bond Street, the first exhibition was held, the members consisting of W. F. Wells, Geo. Barrett Jr., William Havell, Francis Nicholson, W. H. Pyne, Joshua Cristall, Robert Hills, S. Rigaud, John and Christopher Varley, W. S. Gilpin, J. Holworthy, S. Shelley, John Glover, J. C. Nattes and Nicholas Pocock. The work of some of these has already been discussed, and it is essential here to say something about the work of the rest. John Varley (1778–1842) may be considered to be the 'Grand Old Man' of water-colour painting, numbering among his pupils such artists as David Cox, W. H. Hunt, Turner of Oxford, Peter De Wint, Copley Fielding and John Linnell. His output—700 drawings to the Old Society alone—inevitably means that some of his work is repetitive and quality varies a great deal, though it was always of a high technical standard, if sometimes rather hard. He is seen at his best, perhaps, in his Thames drawings, which are pleasingly placid and restful, and in his beautifully drawn, sparingly tinted drawings of Welsh border streets and buildings, whereas, especially in later life, he relied more and more upon a stock vocabulary, as it were, of distant mountains, a placid lake, a tall tree to one side leaning inwards and a foreground with one or two figures gazing out across the water, such as in his typical 'Snowdon' (Manchester Art Gallery). We should bear in mind his tricks of using gum in some of his shadows and of painting upon thin paper laid on a white card through which he could scratch out highlights. Many of Varley's lesser drawings consist

JOHN VARLEY (1778–1842)
On the Thames

of well-placed masses of colour with hardly any pencil drawing, but with much use of thin white lines between them, and it is assumed that these were 'teaching drawings' intended for study and copying by his pupils. His brother Cornelius (1781–1873) could at times be his equal, particularly in his drawings of streets and buildings, using clean washes of clear colour effectively. The effect he obtained is often reminiscent of Cotman's work. A third brother, William Fleetwood (1785–1856), is lesser known, though at times his work, usually rather pretty, would rival that of Cornelius.

George Barrett Jr. (1767–1842) was an artist whose work is usually immediately recognisable by its rich browns, oranges and purple-browns, associated characteristically with glowing, translucent sunrises and sunsets. We usually find large leaves of burdock in the foreground, some kind of ruined Grecian temple and a shepherd tending sheep or goats. His work often resembles that of his fellow member Joshua Cristall (*c.* 1767–1847), who at one time decorated porcelain at Caughley in Shropshire. He painted genre subjects, usually featuring country maidens, accurately drawn, and delicately tinted in mauve-pink, clear yellow-green and grey-blue, with foliage hinted at rather than drawn, with the brush without any pencil. An artist whose work often resembles even more closely that of Barrett was Francis Oliver Finch (1802–62). A noted early collaborator with Barrett was Frederick Tayler (1802–89), a pupil of Richard Sasse (1774–1849) and a fine painter of sporting, pastoral and genre subjects, often very much in the style of David Cox. John Glover (1767–1849) travelled in France, Switzerland and Italy, and died in Tasmania, and is best known as the

JOSEPH NASH (1808–78)

A view of St. George's Chapel, Windsor

painter of trees with a split brush—binding together the hairs to make several points, and thus saving time and effort. The resultant characteristic rendering of trees and bushes is often associated with his method of suggesting slanting evening light by little glints of white. Many Glover drawings are badly faded, because in common with many other water-colourists of his day he mixed together indigo and indian red for his skies. The name of William Havell (1782–1857) is usually associated with views on the Thames, but he was in fact widely travelled and prolific. His work is painstaking, usually with an abundance of trees in full foliage rendered in dark tones of brown, green and purple-grey.

Francis Nicholson (1753–1844) has already been mentioned as the inventor of a method of painting foliage, and another of his short cuts was to duplicate outline drawing by means of taking blacklead impressions from an etched plate, which he then washed in. His water-colours incline to be woolly and were usually painted in a rather monotonous, soft range of yellowish greens and browns, with indian red and indigo skies which, like Glover's, have usually faded to pale red. He was fond of mountainous views, usually with a waterfall, in the Lake District, Yorkshire, Wales and Scotland. William Henry Pyne (1769–1843), author and landscape painter, was an able figure-painter, and figures usually play an important part in his drawings. The treasurer of the Society was Samuel Shelley (*c.* 1750–1808), primarily a miniature painter, whose water-colours were often illustrations of poetic themes, but whose work apart from some fine miniature portrait studies is not important enough for it to be well known. Much the same may be said of the work of the president, William Sawrey Gilpin (1762–1843), son of Sawrey Gilpin, R.A., and nephew of the Rev. William Gilpin, though the reason here may well be that very few examples of it are represented in the public collections. The man chosen to be secretary, however, Robert Hills (1769–1844), is a familiar figure to every collector, not only because his output was large (600 drawings at the Society) but also because of his remarkable ability as a painter of farmyards, rustic lanes and animals. Such was his keen observation that a farmer is easily able to recognise the breed of his cattle and sheep, and sometimes he painted deer. There is considerable difference between his earlier and later work. Until about 1810 his landscapes and studies of winding lanes overhung with trees are full of light, spacious, low-toned in colour, and much more carefully drawn than his later work, which is rendered in hot, reddish tones, woolly and with foliage more quickly and even crudely drawn. Hills' animals are sometimes seen in landscapes by G. F. Robson (1788–1833).

Of the other founder members of the 'Old Society', Nicholas Pocock has already been mentioned, and Stephen Francis Rigaud (1777–1861) and John Claude Nattes (*c.* 1765–1822) contributed comparatively little to the development of the art. William Frederick Wells (1762–1836), however, though not well known, deserves better recognition. He was a close friend of Turner and collaborator of John Laporte (1761–1839) in the making of soft-ground etchings after drawings by Gainsborough. A sketch inscribed 'Rothamurchus' on the reverse, and signed, in my possession shows his typical drawing in very soft pencil, with much cross-hatching and variously spaced line shading, the foreground tree outlines looped or sharply zigzagged and the distant ones done with long, curved lines. This particular drawing is washed in thinly with yellow-green and pale grey. Wells was fond of painting rustic scenes with cottages and children in a palette of subdued but yet colourful tones, the whole having a soft appearance, and with much use of long, curving brush strokes in trees and bushes.

The success of the 'Old Society' encouraged the founding of others, 'The New Society of Painters in Miniature and Water-colours' in 1807, 'The Associated Artists in Water-colours' in 1808 and the 'Royal Institute of Painters in Water-colours' in 1831, while many painters who worked both in oils and in water-colours continued to exhibit at the Academy.

Joseph Mallord William Turner, R.A. (1775–1851) exhibited 259 works at the Academy between 1790 and 1850. For a time he worked with Girtin under Dr. Monro's direction, but it was after his friend's early death that foreign landscape, particularly Alpine, inspired Turner to study the effects of light, which increasingly influenced his style, to culminate in the delicate, ethereal blues, reds, pinks and yellows of his later years. At the same time, while his fame rests upon his inimitable ability to represent every mood of nature in glowing colour on Whatman's paper, it must not be forgotten that in his earlier work he showed an accuracy and delicacy of drawing that has seldom been equalled. William Delamotte (1775–1863), born in the same year as Turner and Girtin, painted in a manner reminiscent of the former's early style, his subjects being mainly views in England, Wales and Switzerland. Though much less flamboyant in their colouring, David Cox (1783–1859), pupil of the Birmingham artist Joseph Barber (1757–1811), and Peter de Wint (1784–1849) must be classed with Turner in their ability to represent Nature in water-colour, though there is considerable difference between the ways in which they worked. De Wint loved quiet colour, though in fact the almost sombre schemes of the flat, open scenes in which he delighted are based upon intense, radiant tones. He used solidly massed forms to depict his shallow panoramas of rich valleys with slow-moving rivers, and seldom paid very much attention to the skies above. Cox, on the other hand, seems to have seized primarily upon the effects of cloud in all its forms, calm or tempestuous, as the key to his compositions. True, while he was at Hereford between 1814 and 1827 he painted quiet pastoral scenes which he sold to make his living, but during that time his introduction to Wales, and particularly the district around Bettws-y-Coed, had the effect of loosening and broadening his work. So, after about 1830, he began to paint the wild mountain and moorland scenes, the angry tempestuous skies, which are typical Cox to most collectors. He returned finally to his birth place, Birmingham, in 1841, and though his failing eyesight is betrayed by a certain loss of detail, his drawings of this period are of great power and beauty, and perhaps the finest he ever did.

During the period under discussion schools of painting grew up in many parts of the country, and notably in East Anglia around Norwich, where in 1803 the 'Norwich Society' was founded, of which John Crome ('Old Crome') was president. Crome painted rarely in water-colour, and our attention must be given to the work of John Sell Cotman (1782–1842), whose water-colours are comparable with those of Francis Towne in that both men made effective use of patterned areas of flat colour. Cotman made a practice of leaving lighter spaces of paper or of his first wash upon which details of shipping or stonework, for instance, were drawn in with scrupulous care. John Thirtle (1777–1839) owed much to Cotman, his brother-in-law, and his rather slight studies are delicately drawn and spontaneous. It must be noted that John Constable (1776–1837) was a water-colourist, and many of his preliminary sketches in the medium are extremely beautiful. It is convenient here to mention Paul Sandby Munn (1775–1845), godson of Paul Sandby, who worked with Cotman and who painted extremely delicate landscapes, though his work is usually seen in the form of views of water-mills, ruins, farmyards and

GEORGE FENNELL ROBSON (1788–1833)

A view of Hereford

cottages drawn in pencil and washed in with monochrome or with rather pale, insipid colours.

A minor school grew up in Bath around the Barker
brothers, Benjamin (1776–1838) and Thomas (1769–
1847). The latter is usually known as 'Barker of
Bath', and though he painted mainly in oils, his
water-colours are effective in a rather woolly manner,
with characteristic wiped-out lights in his foliage,
scratched-out lights in the water and gummed shadows. Benjamin was also a landscape painter, very
much in the same style, with a preference for browns,
yellows, greens and greys.

It has been noted that among those who came under
the influence of John Varley were George Fennell
Robson (1788–1833) and A. V. Copley Fielding

(1787–1855). As the result of an extended Scottish tour, most of Robson's drawings are of Scottish views and very often of river valleys, of which he seems to have been particularly fond. These, and river scenes in other parts of the country (for among the best of his work which I have seen are charming drawings of Hereford Bridge and London Bridge), he painted in translucent browns and yellowish greens with trees rather mechanically rendered in woolly clumps. The sheep or cattle placed in these charac- teristically soft, restful drawings were sometimes painted by Robert Hills. So completely did Copley Fielding absorb the principles of Varley's typical composition that most of his earlier drawings, save for a different treatment of trees, might excusably be wrongly attributed, particularly since the same sub- jects were often painted by both, possibly at the same time. This early phase of Fielding's work was followed by the painting of seascapes and coastal views, and in his latter years, when his subjects were found in Sussex, his style became much looser though more painstaking, with a penchant for mysterious, low-lying mists across fields and over water. Indeed, anyone familiar with Copley Fielding's early, rather hard work might well be excused if he failed to iden- tify the later, though it was usually signed. A con- temporary landscapist whose water-colours are seldom seen in their original state, due to fading, is William Payne (*fl.* 1776–1803), notably a painter of picturesque views of Devon, but who also worked in Wales (after 1809) and the Lake District (after 1811).

An unfaded drawing by him shows a great deal of blue and Payne's grey (his own invention), but the overall effect of the drawings we usually see is one of sombre orange and grey. Payne's figures are unmistakable, washed in with the brush, and often almost transparent, like shadows.

A quite different effect of subdued, rather monotonous tone, in this case of grey and yellowish green, is to be seen in much of the somewhat woolly, but nevertheless entirely appealing in a restful kind of way, topographical drawing of James Bourne (1773–1854).

Among architectural water-colourists the name of Samuel Prout (1783–1852) is best known, though his earlier coastal scenes and groups of cottages are perhaps to some the more attractive. It was during visits to the Continent that he developed his love for old buildings, which, by and large, he rendered in brown ink and brownish wash for near objects and blue ink and blue wash for the distant, a method which, incidentally, was used also by William Callow and Turner of Oxford to good effect. It was at this time that Prout developed his well-known 'broken-line' treatment, which he used to indicate the lines of decaying stonework. Samuel's nephew, John Skinner Prout (1806–76), painted in a similar manner, particularly in his drawings of old Bristol, but was inclined to use splashes of bright colour. The accurate representation of old Continental buildings was still so much in demand that many water-colourists specialised in it, including Charles Wild (1781–1835),

55

JOHN SKINNER PROUT (1806–76)

Church Interior at Caudebec, on the Seine

pupil of Thomas Malton, Henry Edridge (1769–1821), a noted portrait painter but at times superior to Prout in his rather rare architectural drawings, Frederick Nash (1782–1856), Joseph Nash (1808–78), a pupil of Pugin, Samuel Read (1815–83) and Thomas Colman Dibdin (1810–93). Though James Duffield Harding (1797–1863) is better known for his landscape painting and particularly for his skill in painting trees, he often equalled Prout, from whom he had lessons, when he tried his hand at an occasional large architectural drawing.

Among the later topographers whose treatment of town views and picturesque architecture is outstanding we have space here to mention but a few. Richard Parkes Bonington (1802–28 must stand first by reason of sheer technical brilliance, though at times he was equalled by William Callow (1812–1908) and James Holland (1800–1870). He was a master of what is called the 'broken wash', of the use, that is, of a wash of just the right 'wetness' to make full use of the irregularities of the paper. His compositions are always faultless, and the delicacy of his figure drawing outstanding. William Callow met Thomas Shotter Boys (1804–74), pupil of Bonington, in Paris, and from him caught a love of picturesque street scenes which he rendered, with many fine landscapes, and a fine sense of colour, though his figure drawing is apt to be impressionistic rather than accurate. James Holland is best known for his Venetian studies, rich yet restrained, and David Roberts (1796–1864) for his careful, firm pencil drawing of Continental scenes, lightly tinted. J. Scarlett Davis (*c.* 1804–44), whose drawings are rare, drew interiors which are remarkable for delicately graduated pencil line and delicate colour.

Edward Lear (1812–88) had the same facility for brilliant drawing, often full of minute detail, coupled with warm, often neutral colouring, and his work, much of which was done around the Mediterranean, was sketched on the spot, titled and dated, and scribbled over with notes to help with the colouring, which was done later.

When we move on to painters of ships and shipping the name of William Clarkson Stanfield (1793–1867)

WILLIAM CALLOW (1812–1908)

Richmond Castle, Yorkshire

springs immediately to mind. In his day, working at one time with David Roberts, he was famous as a scenery painter at Drury Lane, but a period as a sailor between 1808 and 1818 gave him a store of knowledge of the details of ships and a love for the sea which caused him to become a seacape painter above all else. The colour of Clarkson Stanfield's sea is always in keeping with the weather conditions, his waves and the movements of his ships always governed precisely by the direction of the wind, and his water always real water, whether out at sea, calm as a millpond in a harbour or in a rocky coastal pool. His coastal scenes, with boats drawn up on the beach and containing many accurately drawn figures, are perhaps the most attractive of all his work, though an occasional miniature drawing may glow like a jewel. Samuel Owen (1768–1857), Samuel Austin (1796–1834), William and John Cantiloe Joy (born at Yarmouth in 1803 and 1806 respectively), James Wilson Carmichael (1800–68), George Chambers (1803–40), Charles Bentley (1806–54) and William Adolphus Knell (*c*. 1825–75) are other outstanding contemporary water-colourists of marine subjects, and if we add the name of Thomas Bush Hardy (1842–97) it is because although he was highly esteemed in his day yet is now usually looked upon as a painter of mediocre pot-boilers, he could on occasion produce a miniature harbour scene which, if it were not signed (as practically all his water-colours are), would by reason of its exquisite drawing and lovely colour be attributed to greater men.

An important phase of water-colour drawing during the nineteenth century was book illustration, particularly as regards figure studies of historical, fictional or sentimental kinds. Thomas Stothard (1755–1834), some of whose illustrations were cut in wood by Luke Clennell (1781–1840), himself a talented water-colourist of genre subjects, forms a link between the earlier and later men in this regard, as, of course, does the inimitable caricaturist Thomas Rowlandson (1756–1827), imitations of whose work are to be found everywhere. William Blake (1757–1827) was almost exactly contemporary with Rowlandson, but his work shows clearly the difference between the two men, the visionary and the earthy caricaturist, the poet and the cynical observer of, often, the more sordid side of human nature. Blake was capable, above all, of expressing, dramatically, every human emotion in sinuous, flowing line. Of the later men there was William Henry Hunt (1790–1864), better known as 'Birds' Nest Hunt' for his groups of fruit and birds' nests, though his lesser known studies of rustic figures are of much greater importance. For these Hunt used the stipple technique, as, of course, did Miles Birket Foster (1825–99), though on a much smaller scale. At the other extreme Louis Haghe (1806–85) drew his accurate groups of Dutch soldiers and burghers and his meticulously rendered church interiors in gouache, with clever effects of lighting, and George Cattermole (1800–68) used his vast knowledge of medieval architecture and costume to good effect in his strictly

accurate and picturesque scenes from history and
Shakespeare. William James Müller (1812–45), apprentice of James Baker Pyne (1800–70) and David
Cox's teacher of oil-painting, was first and foremost
a landscapist in the Turner atmospheric tradition,
but he also painted an occasional interior of the
romantic kind, with a dramatic lighting effect and
figures. The fame of John Frederick Lewis (1805–76)
rests, above all, on his Eastern figure drawings,
among which 'The Hareem' (Victoria and Albert
Museum) is an outstanding example. William Daniell
(1769–1837) went with his uncle Thomas to the Far
East in 1786, as a result of which they exhibited many
Indian views at the Royal Academy and elsewhere,
but he is best known for his broad, Girtin-like
English drawings. George Chinnery (1774–1865), on
the other hand, also voyaged to the East, but to
India, where his father had been a Madras merchant,
and he remained there for some time before moving
finally to China. His bold, tinted pen drawings of
shipping subjects in particular are outstanding.

In this chapter many famous names have perforce
been omitted, and it is only natural that some of them
must spring to mind as we remember drawings that
have given pleasure. William Leighton Leitch (1804–
83), for example, may go down in history as Queen
Victoria's teacher, but he could be as good as David
Roberts, and in almost every example of his drawings
in the purest of water-colour there is always one
small area which, if magnified, would be a perfect
miniature in itself. One thinks back to David Cox,

DAVID ROBERTS (1796–1864)

Yaffa, Ancient Joppa

and the mind recalls the work of Thomas Collier (1840–1901) with his windswept moors, of Edmund M. Wimperis (1835–1900), painter of peat-bogs and lonely mountainsides, and of Edwin Hayes (1820–1904), who drew low-lying marshland. And what of William Turner of Oxford (1789–1862), who may well have outclassed all his contemporaries had he not chosen instead to live out a comfortable life as a drawing master? There is indeed no end to one's choice, which in any event must in the last resort be biased by personal taste.

SIR E. C. BURNE-JONES

(1833–98)

Sidonia von Borke

5

THE EARLY TWENTIETH CENTURY

IT is too early yet to assess the importance which will be given to twentieth-century water-colour by posterity. There have been so many external influences, so many interpretations of the aesthetic and so much breaking away from tradition that it is impossible to know what will last and what may be ephemeral.

Landscape has always been the main preoccupation of the water-colour painter, but whereas the early masters of the art, encouraged by pride of estate and avid enthusiasm for travel, looked above all for the 'picturesque', for the suitably sublime, towards the end of the nineteenth century a new spirit was abroad, a search for the underlying emotional or moral effect which a painting could have upon the viewer. John Ruskin (1819–1900), ruthless critic and staunch supporter of the Pre-Raphaelite movement, painted powerful water-colours, and his teaching was largely responsible for the new approach, while Philip Wilson Steer (1860–1942), steeped in the French Impressionist insistence upon the free expression of what is seen by the mind's inner eye, handled his water-colour so as to give swift, delicate glimpses of atmosphere, tone and form, with here and there a hint of Cozens' 'blots' and Turner's diaphanous mists. The Impressionist school was indeed encouraged by the founding of the 'New English Art Club', which held its first Exhibition in 1866, the aim of its members being to paint Nature brilliantly in rapid effects. Hercules Brabazon Brabazon (né Sharpe, 1821–1906) was a prominent member, and his work is characterised by swift brushwork, relying entirely upon broad washes with scarcely any pencil assistance.

This analysis of the effects of light and atmosphere was not the only preoccupation of the early-twentieth-century water-colourist. In quite a different sphere, while H. W. Nevison painted in oil the guns and gunners of the First World War, Paul Nash (1889–1946) recorded its horrors in water-colour in a cubist form which he later adapted to the abstract. Other war-time water-colourists were Graham Sutherland and John Piper, both born in 1903, the former recording in his flat patterns, restless line and fiery colour the effects of gunfire and bomb, and the glow of munition factories and the latter, in more sombre tones, the aftermath of blitzkrieg. Piper is well known also for his series of drawings of Windsor, topographical but somehow desolate in a romantic kind of way. Henry Moore also makes brilliant use of water-colour, as evidenced in his 'shelter' drawings of 1941.

It is, of course, always tempting to try to see in the work of later water-colourists the influence of their predecessors, and in fact early traditions have never been entirely cast to one side, though inevitably they have been approached from a different aesthetic point of view. Piper, David Jones and Frances Hodgkins (1871–1947) belonged to a body of artists who, like Samuel Palmer before them, continued to paint in the romantic tradition, but introduced into their work modern conceptions of form. A. W. Rich (1856–1921) was the modern disciple of De Wint as

DANTE GABRIEL ROSSETTI (1828–82)

How Sir Galahad, Sir Bors and Sir Percival were fed with the Sancgreal; but Sir Percival's Sister died by the way

J. D. Innes (1887–1914) sometimes was of Cotman, many of the illustrations painted by Kate Greenaway (1846–1901), with their delightful studies of children, are as appealing to us as they were to our grand-parents, and the stipplings of Albert Goodwin (1845–1932) are comparable to those of Birket Foster, though in them he attained a sense of mystery and of poetic fantasy that is far removed from the latter's accomplished, careful prettiness, and is indeed often reminiscent of Turner. Frederick Goodall (1822–1904) worked at first in the manner of David Wilkie, depicting scenes of village life, but went on to rival Edward Matthew Ward (1816–79) in his accurately colourful Biblical and historical subjects.

I can perhaps best end this necessarily short chapter, and indeed the book itself, by suggesting that the study of English water-colours is, above all, a study of the work of individuals and their own individual methods. Though every teacher passed on to his pupils some of his own style (as did John Varley to Copley Fielding, for example), every drawing is a personal thing, and it is difficult to ascribe it to any particular 'school'. For this reason apology is made to those readers who may be disappointed or surprised by reason of omissions. My hope is that enough has been said to whet the appetite and to encourage not only further reading but also many hours of pleasure in our Art Galleries.

BIBLIOGRAPHY

THE books listed below have been found to be useful in the preparation of this book. It is true that some titles are out of print, but they are not that difficult to obtain, and are certainly not of too high a price to buy. The reader who wishes to pursue his reading and researches should consult the excellent bibliography in Martin Hardie's *Water-colour Painting in Britain*, Vol. III, 1968.

1. BALDRY, A. L. *British Marine Painting*, 1919.
2. BALDRY, A. L. 'William Turner of Oxford' (*Walker's Quarterly*, No. 11, 1922–23).
3. BELL, C. F. 'John Sell Cotman' (*Walker's Quarterly*, Nos. 19–20, 1926).
4. BELL, C. F. 'Miles Edmund Cotman' (*Walker's Quarterly*, No. 21, 1927).
5. BINYON, L. *English Water-colours*, 1933–45.
6. BRYAN, M. *Dictionary of Painters and Engravers*, 1903.
7. BUNT, C. A. *David Cox*, 1946.
8. BUNT, C. G. E. *Little Masters of English Land-scape*, 1949.
9. BURY, A. *Francis Towne*, 1962.
10. CLIFFORD, D. *Watercolours of the Norwich School*, 1965.
11. CUNDALL, H. M. *Birket Foster*, 1906.
12. CUNDALL, H. M. *Masters of the Water-colour Painting*, 1922.

13. CUNDALL, H. M. *The Norwich School*, 1920.
14. CUNNINGHAM, A. *The Lives of the Most Eminent Painters*, 1929–32.
15. DAVIDSON, A. *Edward Lear*, 1938.
16. DAVIES, R. *Chats on Old English Drawing*, 1923.
17. DICKES, W. F. *The Norwich School of Painting*, 1905.
18. EMANUEL, F. L. 'William Callow' (*Walker's Quarterly*, No. 22, 1927).
19. EMANUEL, F. L. 'William Roxby Beverley' (*Walker's Quarterly*, No. 2, 1920–21).
20. FINBERG, A. J. *Life of J. M. W. Turner*, 1939.
21. FINBERG, A. J. *The English Water-colour Painters*, 1905.
22. GILCHRIST, *A Life of William Blake*, 1945.
23. GIRTIN, T. and LOSHAK, D. *The Art of Thomas Girtin*, 1954.
24. GRANT, M. H. *Dictionary of British Landscape Painters*, 1952.
25. GRAVES, A. *Dictionary of Artists 1760–1893*, 1901–69.
26. HARDIE, M. *Peter de Wint*, 1929.
27. HARDIE, M. and CLAYTON, M. 'Thomas Daniell and William Daniell' (*Walker's Quarterly*, Nos. 35-36, 1932).
28. HARDIE, M. *Water-colour Painting in Britain*, 1967–69.
29. HEINTZELMAN, A. W. *Water-colour Drawings of Thomas Rowlandson*, 1947.
30. HENDERSON, E. L. K. *Morland and Ibbetson*, 1923.

31. HOLME, C. *The Royal Institute of Painters in Water-colour*, 1906.
32. HUGHES, C. E. *Early English Watercolour*, 1913–15.
33. HUISH, M. B. *British Water-colour Art*, 1904.
34. KITSON, S. D. *Life of John Sell Cotman*, 1937.
35. LOCK, H. R. 'Alfred William Rich' (*Walker's Quarterly*, No. 9, 1922–23).
36. LONG, B. S. 'Francis Nicholson' (*Walker's Quarterly*, No. 14, 1923–24).
37. Long, B. S. 'John Laporte and P. La Cave' (*Walker's Quarterly*, No. 8, 1921–22).
38. LONG, B. S. 'John (Warwick) Smith' (*Walker's Quarterly*, No. 24, 1927).
39. LONG, B. S. 'William Payne' (*Walker's Quarterly*, No. 6, 1921–22).
40. MAAS, J. *Victorian Painters*, 1968.
41. MACCOLL, D. S. *Philip Wilson Steer*, 1945.
42. OPPÉ, A. P. *Alexander and J. R. Cozens*, 1952.
43. OPPÉ, A. P. *The Water-colours of Turner, Cox, De Wint*, 1925.
44. OPPÉ, A. P. *Water-colours of Turner*, 1925.
45. PALMER, A. H. *Life and Laters of Samuel Palmer*, 1892.
46. QUIGLEY, J. 'David Roberts' (*Walker's Quarterly*, No. 10, 1922–23).
47. QUIGLEY, J. *Prout and Roberts*, 1926.
48. REDGRAVE, G. R. *A History of Water-colour Painting in England*, 1892
49. REDGRAVE, R. and S. *A Century of British Painters*, 1866–1947.

50. REYNOLDS, E. P. 'Claude Hayes' (*Walker's Quarterly*, No. 7, 1921–22).
51. REYNOLDS, G. *Victorian Painting*, 1966.
52. RICH, A. W. *Water-colour Painting*, 1918.
53. ROE, F. G. 'Henry Bright of the Norwich School' (*Walker's Quarterly*, No. 1, 1920–21).
54. ROGET, J. L. *A History of the Old Water-colour Society*, 1891.
55. SANDBY, W. *The History of the Royal Academy of Arts*, 1862.
56. SMITH, S. C. K. *Crome*, 1923.
57. STOKES, H. *Girtin and Bonnington*, 1922.
58. STOKES, H. 'James Holland' (*Walker's Quarterly*, No. 23, 1927).
59. STOKES, H. 'Thomas Shotter Boys' (*Walker's Quarterly*, No. 18, 1926).
60. STORY, A. T. *James Holmes and John Varley*, 1894.
61. THOMSON, D. Croal *The Water-colour Drawings of Thomas Bewick*, 1930.
62. THORNBURY, G. W. *Life of J. M. W. Turner*, 1862–1970.
63. WEDMORE, Sir F. *English Water-colour*, 1902.
64. WEDMORE, Sir F. *Hercules Brabazon Brabazon*, 1913.
65. WHITLEY, W. T. *Art in England*, 1928, 1929.
66. WILENSKI, R. H. *English Painting*, 1964.
67. WILLIAMS, IOLO *Early English Water-colours*, 1952.
68. WIMPERIS, E. 'Edmund Morison Wimperis, R.I.' (*Walker's Quarterly*, No. 3, 1920–21).

Much essential and valuable information is contained in the following publications, especially museum and art-gallery catalogues of particular collections.

1. Annual Volumes of the Old Water-colour Society.
2. Annual Volumes of the Walpole Society.
3. *Catalogue of Pictures and Drawings at Harwell House*, 1936.
4. *Catalogue of the Sale Bequest of Water-colours*, Victoria Institute, Worcester.
5. *Catalogue of Water-colours and Drawings*, 1957, National Gallery, Edinburgh.
6. *Catalogue of Water-colour Painting by British Artists* (National Gallery of British Art, Victoria and Albert Museum), 1908, 1927, Supplement 1951.
7. *Early English Drawings and Water-colours*, 1968, Walker Art Gallery, Liverpool.
8. *Early English Water-colours*, 1966, City Art Gallery, Sheffield.
9. *Early Water-colours from the Collection of Thomas Girtin*, 1953, Graves Art Gallery, Sheffield.
10. *English Drawings and Water-colours from the Collection of Mr. and Mrs. Paul Mellon*, 1964–65, Colnaghi.
11. *Illustrated Catalogue of Water-colour Drawings*, 1938, Laing Art Gallery, Newcastle.
12. *Illustrated Guide to the Collection of Norwich School Painters*, 1951, Castle Museum, Norwich.
13. *Illustrations of One Hundred Water-colours*, 1953, Art Gallery, Birmingham.

14. *Masters of British Water-colours, 17th-19th Century*, 1949, Royal Academy.
15. *The British Water-colour School*, 1939, National Museum of Wales, Cardiff.
16. *Water-colours from the Gilbert Davies Collection*, 1949, 1955, Arts Council.

The following periodicals carry articles on water-colour painting, painters, collecting and prices. Back numbers of these are also well worth buying, especially early issues of *Studio*.

1. *Antique Dealer and Collector's Guide* (monthly).
2. *Antique Collector* (bi-monthly).
3. *Apollo* (monthly).
4. *Art and Antiques Weekly* (weekly).
5. *Art and Artists* (monthly).
6. *Art Prices Current* (annually).
7. *Arts Review* (fortnightly).
8. *Studio International* (monthly).
9. *The Burlington Magazine* (monthly).
10. *The Connoisseur* (monthly).

ENGLISH WATER-COLOURS IN PUBLIC COLLECTIONS

THERE are few public art galleries in Britain without a few examples of water-colours, some have particularly comprehensive collections, while others specialise in the work of one artist, often with local connections. The latter are listed below, and should be visited whenever convenient. Many of the galleries publish their own catalogues, and these are often rich sources of reference on the work and lives of artists—frequently they are the only source.

ABERDEEN: Art Gallery and Regional Museum
ACCRINGTON: Haworth Art Gallery
BATH: Victoria Art Gallery
BEDFORD: Cecil Higgins Art Gallery
BELFAST: Ulster Museum
BIRKENHEAD: Williamson Art Gallery and Museum
BIRMINGHAM: City Museum and Art Gallery
BOLTON: Museum and Art Gallery
BOURNEMOUTH: Russell-Cotes Art Gallery and Museum
BRIGHTON: Art Gallery and Museum
BRISTOL: Museum and Art Gallery
BURNLEY: Towneley Art Gallery and Museum
CARDIFF: The National Museum of Wales
CHELTENHAM: Art Gallery and Museum
DONCASTER: Museum and Art Gallery

DUBLIN: Museum of Science and Art
DUNDEE: Orchar Art Gallery
EXETER: Royal Albert Memorial Museum and Art Gallery
HARROGATE: Corporation Art Gallery
HEREFORD: Churchill Gardens Museum
IPSWICH: Christchurch Mansion
LEEDS: City Art Gallery
LEICESTER: Museum and Art Gallery
LINCOLN: Usher Gallery
LIVERPOOL: Walker Art Gallery
LONDON:
  British Museum
  Victoria and Albert Museum
  National Maritime Museum
  Tate Gallery
  Courtauld Institute of Art
MANCHESTER: Whitworth Art Gallery
MELBOURNE (AUSTRALIA): National Gallery of Victoria
NEWCASTLE UPON TYNE:
  Laing Art Gallery
  Higham Palace Gallery
NEWPORT (MONMOUTH): Museum and Art Gallery
NORWICH: Castle Museum
NOTTINGHAM: City Art Gallery
OXFORD: The Ashmolean Museum
PHILADELPHIA (U.S.A.): Academy of Fine Arts
PLYMOUTH: City Museum and Art Gallery
PORT SUNLIGHT (CHESHIRE): The Lady Lever Art Gallery

PRESTON: Harris Museum and Art Gallery
ROCHDALE: Art Gallery and Museum
SHEFFIELD: Graves Art Gallery
STOCKPORT: War Memorial Art Gallery
STOKE-ON-TRENT: City Museum and Art Gallery
WAKEFIELD: City Art Gallery
WARRINGTON: Municipal Museum and Art Gallery
WHITBY: Whitby Art Gallery
WOLVERHAMPTON: Municipal Art Gallery and Museum
WORCESTER: City Museum and Art Gallery
YORK: City of York Art Gallery

PART II

*A Historical
Sequence
of
Water-colours*

Note: **S.** signifies signed and **D.** dated.

1 JOHN BAPTIST CLAUDE CHATELAIN (1710–71)

Classical Composition [$8\frac{3}{4} \times 11\frac{7}{8}$ ins.]: S. and D.

A typical pen drawing washed in with pale water-colour, in
this case grey for the background and a brown foreground.
Also typical are the castles perched on the crags, the
stream and the sketched-in figures. The drawing is, of
course, imaginary, but Chatelain also did a number of topographical views. Though he was born and died in London, his
parents were French and his real name was Philippe.

79

2 ALEXANDER COZENS c. 1717–86)

Landscape with Rivers and Mountains [$6\frac{1}{2} \times 8\frac{1}{4}$ ins.]

This water-colour drawing is an example of how Cozens was able to suggest a wide expanse of countryside in a very small area. Though he was widely known—and abused—for his method of constructing a drawing around a series of 'blots' (as described in his pamphlet *A New Method for Assisting the Invention in the Composition of Landscape*), he was nevertheless an outstanding master of imaginative landscape.

3 COPLESTONE WARRE BAMPFYLDE (1720–91)

Coastal View through an Archway [13¼ × 10¾ ins.]

Though better known as an amateur caricaturist, Bampfylde was also a landscape painter, who exhibited at the Royal Academy and elsewhere between 1763 and 1783. This drawing. washed in with the typical blue-greens of the period, is a topographical one in the manner of Paul Sandby, by whom Bampfylde was much influenced.

4 PAUL SANDBY (*c.* 1725–1809)
An Ancient Beech Tree [27⅝ × 41⅝ ins.]
S. and D. 1794

Paul Sandby is usually thought of as a
topographer, and indeed he was responsible
for introducing many of the beauties of
outlying places to his generation,
often in a delightfully picturesque manner.
At the same time, he was often inspired
by some particular object the intrinsic
beauty of which obliged him to paint it.
This drawing, in body-colour as are many
of his drawings, is a case in point,
for Sandby was particularly fond of
trees, for which he clearly had a complete
understanding, doubtless acquired during
his observations in Windsor Great Park.
Apart from the outstanding feature of the
great tree-trunk, we note the fine
rendering of distance, the perfect placing
and grouping of the figures, and the
careful pencilling of the foreground.

5 THOMAS GAINSBOROUGH (1727–88)

Landscape with Archway of Rock [12 × 16 ins.]

A drawing in distemper washed with gum, which shows a break-away from mere topographical drawing to something of a more poetical, romantic nature, a movement furthered by Gainsborough and Richard Wilson in particular. In fact, it is probably just the kind of drawing which served as an example to such young artists as Girtin, Turner and John Varley when they studied at Dr. Monro's Adelphi Terrace 'Academy'. Apart from the obvious vigour of the drawing, the diagonal brushwork typical of Gainsborough's work of this kind is clearly visible.

6 THOMAS GAINSBOROUGH (1727–88)

Rubbing down the Mare [18⅝ × 13½ ins.]

A drawing in pencil, pen, black chalk
and washes of brown, blue and yellow,
inspired by that close observation of
country scenes which was the source of
much of Gainsborough's work. We notice
the typical diagonal lines of shading,
but above all we see the masterly
economy of effort, the faithful rendering
of the reaction of the mare to the
attentions of her groom and his to her
restiveness, and invariably the
beautiful firm drawing.

7 ANTHONY DEVIS (1729–1816)

A View of London from Dulwich [11⅝ × 16 ins.]

A drawing in pencil and washes of blue-green and pale yellow
strengthened with pen which probably dates from about 1770,
when Devis was drawing finished, often quite large topographical works. The same characteristic rendering of foliage
by a series of loops, like bunches of bananas, which is so
often clearly seen in the many unfinished sketches by this
artist, is visible in the foreground trees.

8 FRANCIS GROSE (*c.* 1731–91)

The Walls of Conway [7 × 20 ins.]

Francis Grose is representative of eighteenth-century amateurs who
loved to draw antiquities—he published a number of books on
the subject, including *Antiquities of England and Wales* in
four volumes, between 1773 and 1787, which were illustrated
by his drawings. This example, drawn with a reed pen and
lightly tinted, shows his usual style of not very accomplished
rendering of stonework, foliage and almost empty foreground.

9 SAMUEL HIERONYMUS GRIMM (1733–94)

Composition from Nature [12¾ × 20¼ ins.]

Though Grimm was born in the Alps, after he settled in
England in 1768 he became a most typical English topographer
with a particular liking for the quieter kind of landscape
complete with villages and old houses, ruined abbeys and
slow-winding rivers. In this example, drawn in sepia ink and
tinted with blue-green, sepia and yellow, are seen Grimm's
usual small figures, judiciously placed and full of movement,
and his exceedingly neat penwork, which, in his trees, has
been likened to minute hemstitching.

11 SAWREY GILPIN, R.A. (1733–1807)

Countryman upon a Horse [10¾ × 14 ins.]

This drawing, which like the previous example is probably
one of a series, is tinted in blue and grey over a pencil
outline. Because Gilpin collaborated not only with George
Barrett Sr. but also with Reinagle it is difficult to assess
his real capabilities as a landscape painter.

88

10 SAWREY GILPIN, R.A. (1733–1807)

A Servant of the Hunt [10¾ × 13⅝ in.]

Sawrey Gilpin is usually known to collectors as the younger
brother of the Rev. William Gilpin or else in association
with the work or travel of other better known men. In this
way, perhaps, he has escaped general notice, though admittedly drawings by him are rare, apart from the two or three
horses often to be seen beneath the groups of trees drawn by
George Barrett Sr. with whom he collaborated. The example here
illustrated, however, with that which follows, show that as
an animal painter Sawrey Gilpin holds his own in any company.

12 AMOS GREEN (1735–1807)

River Valley with Bridge [7½ × 9⅞ ins.]

Amos Green, born at Halesowen in Worcestershire, was an amateur landscape water-colourist of the Lake District, where he settled late in life. His work, carried out usually in brown or sepia monochrome with touches of soft green and primrose yellow, is often mistaken for that of the later water-colourist William Green, who also was a Lake District painter. A characteristic touch is the stressing of the trees in the foreground with ink.

13 HARRIET GREEN (*fl. c.* 1780)

View of Alstead and Ingleborough [$5\frac{5}{8} \times 7\frac{3}{4}$ ins.]

The full inscription on the reverse, penned in the artist's
hand, continues . . . 'on leaving Burton in Lonsdale.' The
drawing is an example of the work of the wife of Amos Green,
née Lister, presumably the Miss Lister who exhibited a landscape at the Academy in 1784, much of whose work is very like
that of her husband, who was probably her teacher. It is
always as well to remember that an unsigned drawing attributed
to a master may very well have been painted by a pupil.

14 NICHOLAS POCOCK (1740–1821)

The Wye Bridge, Hereford [16⅜ × 24¼ ins.]: S. and D. 1795

Though Pocock, an ex-sailor, is generally well known as a painter of sea subjects, he often produced pure topography or landscape. This example was possibly made during a tour of South Wales which he is said to have made, a delightfully drawn representation in soft tones of pale yellows and browns of a subject much favoured by water-colourists, including David Cox (cf. *Old Houses, Hereford*, No. 324 in the Birmingham Art Gallery) and G. F. Robson.

15 NICHOLAS POCOCK
(1740–1821)
Ruins [7¾ × 12 ins.]

This is another example of
Pocock's topographical drawing,
carried out in a rather different
style from the previous one.
Pure washes of colour were
applied over shadows washed in
pale grey, and the foliage thickly
outlined with the brush.

16 PHILIP JAMES DE LOUTHERBOURG, R.A. (1740–1812)

The Battle of Camperdown, 11th October 1797 [7¾ × 12 ins.]

Loutherbourg was born in Strasbourg, and came to England in
1771, where he remained. On arrival he became a scenery
designer to Garrick at Drury Lane, and first exhibited at
the Royal Academy in 1772, becoming R.A. in 1781. His
drawings embrace many subjects, including semi-caricatured

theatrical portraits, landscape and shipping, all of them
characterised by pen drawing of great freedom and precision,
and though much of his work was done in sepia or Indian
ink monochrome, his coloured drawings show a highly
developed sense of tone balance, as in this present example,
which is painted in blue, grey and brown, with the large
ship clearly defined against the pale blue smoke of the battle.

17 FRANCIS TOWNE (*c.* 1740–1816)

Landscape with Ruins [14½ × 10¾ ins.]

The high regard in which Towne is held dates back only to
1920, when he was *discovered* by A. P. Oppé. Apparently, the
periods during which he visited Wales (1777), Italy and
Switzerland (1780 and 1781) and the Lake District (1786) had
considerable influence upon his style, so that to neat, flowing pen-work and a fine sense of the value of pure colour was
added greater broadness and brightening of tone. These
characteristics are in fact to be seen in this example, which
may be dated *c.* 1780, though its beauty is badly served by
a photograph in black and white.

18 FRANCIS TOWNE (*c.* 1740–1816)

Part of Ambleside: Morning Effect [6¼ × 9⅜ ins.]

As the title indicates, this drawing is an example of Towne's
Lake District work. It has not quite the power of his best
Italian work, but the boldness of pattern and the contrasts
of simplified colour masses are such that they clearly show
in the photograph, as does the beautifully neat pen-work.

19 JOSEPH CHARLES BARROW (*fl. c.* 1780–1810)

A Gateway in Winchester [14 × 20 ins.]: S. and D. 1800

Hardly anything is known about Barrow—save that the young
John Varley was his assistant and pupil, as was Louis Francia.
His drawings are exceedingly rare, and this pleasing example,
carried out entirely in soft tones of yellows and browns,
shows not only a marked similarity (though perhaps a little
more stilted) to the style of Paul Sandby, but also to that
of Varley in, for example, his Herefordshire drawings. The
drawing is in fact remarkable well done, and one is tempted
to wonder to whom the water-colour might have been attributed
had it not been signed so clearly on the barn door.

20 WILLIAM PARS (1742–82)

View near Simplon at La Valais [$10\frac{1}{2} \times 10\frac{1}{2}$ ins.]

This drawing, delicately penned and tinted in grey, pale blue
and purplish brown, was presumably done at some time before
1771 during a trip to Switzerland and the Tyrol, when Pars
was employed by Lord Palmerston to make drawings for him. It
may be compared for boldness and freedom from fading with the
Italian drawing *On the Tessin, near Poleggio,* which is illustrated in Iolo Williams's *Early English Water-colours.*

100

21 MICHAEL 'ANGELO' ROOKER (1743–1801)

Bury St. Edmunds [9 × 11 ins.]

Rooker's second name was given to him as a joke by Paul Sandby, and thereafter he adopted it, both in his signature and as part of a monogram. As *Signor Rookerini* he was chief scene-painter at the Haymarket Theatre for many years. Drawings such as this, in the architectural style but enlivened with figures, were done during his walking tours in many counties, which he made in order to gather material for his work. A notable feature is the detailed exactitude of his drawing.

22 MICHAEL 'ANGELO' ROOKER (1743–1801)

Kenilworth Castle [9 × 11 ins.]: S.

Rooker was extremely fond of ruins, usually clustered with
bushes and trees. This drawing is in grey monochrome, and
was probably done during a walking tour in Warwickshire. It
should be compared with another drawing of Kenilworth Castle
illustrated by Iolo Williams, which being of the same size,
also in grey monochrome, and treated in exactly the same way,
was probably done at the same time. Note Rooker's characteristic treatment of foliage and sloping banks.

23 THOMAS HEARNE (1744–1817)

St. Botolph's, Colchester [7⅝ × 9⅞ ins.]

A drawing in grey pen and wash, as are so many of Hearne's
best works. Though a little pencil is visible here and there,
most of the drawing was done with the brush. Though Hearne
often painted in limited colour, he may be rated as second
to none in his use of monochrome, when he was able, as in
this example, not only to suggest solidity but also to a
remarkable degree to suggest sunlight shining on the broken
surfaces of old masonry.

24 FRANCIS WHEATLEY, R.A. 1747–1801

*The Volunteers of the City and County of Dublin as they met
on College Green on the 4th November 1779* [16⅞ × 25½ ins.]
An unconventional Wheatley drawing, for he is usually known for his
sentimental renderings of young girls such as the rather insipid, elegant,
and unconvincing street vendors of his *Cries of London* series. In quite
a different style, however, Wheatley was a fine painter of landscape,
cattle and rustic characters which show keen powers of observation.
This last talent was used to good effect in this illustrated example of his
work, which is correct and accurate in detail, even though the figures,
perhaps intentionally, are somewhat wooden. The background in
particular is finely drawn and the whole drawing is tinted.

25 JOHN 'WARWICK' SMITH (1749–1831)

A Welsh Torrent [$6\frac{1}{2} \times 9\frac{3}{4}$ ins.]:
S. and D.

John Smith was given his nickname
because he was patronised
by the second Earl of Warwick,
himself an amateur artist,
who paid for a trip to Italy
which lasted from 1776 to 1781,
when he returned in company with
Francis Towne. This example,
however, was painted during one
of Smith's many trips into
Wales between 1784 and 1806, and
according to the inscription
on the old backing, it is he
himself who is sketching in the
corner. It is delicately drawn in
pencil and lightly washed
in grey, blue and yellowish green.

26 JOHN WEBBER, R.A. (*c.* 1750–93)

Creek, with Figures and Boats [9½ × 13 ins.]

John Webber was a friend of Grimm, son of a Swiss sculptor,
who studied in Berne and in Paris before entering the Academy
Schools in 1775. He accompanied Captain Cook on his last
voyage in 1776, and made a drawing of his death, which he
witnessed. He is naturally best known for his South Sea
scenes, but is at his best in English landscape, which, like
this example, are usually tinted over delicate soft pencil
with washes of soft pale blue, grey and primrose yellow.

108

27 JOHN ROBERT COZENS (*c.* 1752–97)

Shepherd's Hut [10¼ × 14⅝ ins.]

John Robert Cozens was the son of Alexander, and hardly anything is known about his life. Nevertheless, he has always
been a collector's painter who, using a very restricted
palette of greys and blues with only an occasional touch of
brighter colour, was yet able to secure wonderful grandeur
and atmosphere in his water-colours. He visited Italy twice,
and as a result the best known of his drawings are of Italian
scenes. The example chosen is one of the notable exceptions
to his more usual serene style of drawing. It depicts a
dramatic storm scene, and the remarkable sky reminds us that
Cozens was one of the first British artists to make a study
of skies in their every mood.

28 FRANCIS NICHOLSON
(1753–1844)

Coastal Scene with Castle

[19½ × 27 ins.]

A rare example of Nicholson's
work that has not suffered in
any way from fading. If we
substitute a waterfall for the
breaking wave, we have a typical
Nicholson subject, complete
with several interested onlookers,
often tinted in blue,
brown and yellow, as they are
here. Otherwise, the general
colour scheme is in yellow-green
and brown. Nicholson's
treatment of water is generally
very good, and the breaking
wave in this example is extremely
convincing and well done.

110

29 FRANCIS NICHOLSON (1753–1844)

The Bowdar Stone, Borrowdale [13⅛ × 19 ins.]: S. and D. 1808

Nicholson was a Yorkshireman by birth, and most of his
drawings are of Yorkshire subjects, though he painted also
in Wales, Somerset, North Devon, the Lake District and
Scotland. He was the inventor of stopping out highlights
with a mixture of beeswax, flake white and turpentine, which
he did not often use, and his own work, in fact, is
seldom seen to proper advantage, since, despite his inventive-
ness, it is usually badly faded, especially when he used a
mixture of indigo and Indian red for his skies. Here is a
typical example of his style, well composed, and carried out
in browns and yellow-green.

31 THOMAS STOTHARD, R.A.
(1755–1834)

The Three Arts [5¼ × 6¾ ins.]: S.

Stothard had regular employment as a book
illustrator, his style for the most part
being admirably indicated by the titles
of the journals for which he works, such
as the *Poetical Magazine* or the *Lady's
Poetical Magazine*. In other words, he
drew with graceful prettiness that often
became rather formal, whether in pen,
pencil, monochrome or coloured washes.
This is a typical example, beautifully
drawn, with the robes of the women in
typical pale grey, pale brown and pale
blue with a red scarf. It shows one of
Stothard's failings—the eyes of his
figures are unseeing, unfocused, and wide
open, as if they were looking through and
not at the object of their regard.
Although the drawing is signed, it is
well to remember that signatures upon
Stothard drawings are usually forgeries.

30 THOMAS BEWICK
(1753–1828)

*Study of a Black and White
Kingfisher*   [5⅜ × 4⅜ ins.]

The art of wood-engraving was completely
transformed by Bewick, whose lovely little
illustrations in that medium are to be seen in
such of his books as *History of British
Birds*, published in 1797–1804. This drawing
is in Indian ink and water-colour. It is small,
as his bird studies usually are, and shows his
typically neat drawing, particularly of
feathers.

32 SAMUEL HOWITT (1756–1822)

Sandgate, Keeper's House in Windsor Great Park [6¾ × 9½ ins.]: S.

Howitt married Rowlandson's sister, and his early work is
much in the style of early Rowlandsons. This is a typical
example, the outline in pen and the colouring in light tones
of grey, reddish brown and green. A characteristic of Howitt's
drawing, the dog's tooth edging to the foliage, may be clearly
seen, together with the network of branches supporting it,
completely unobscured by leaves.

33 SAMUEL HOWITT (1756–1822)

Extensive Landscape [$7\frac{1}{4} \times 10\frac{1}{4}$ ins.]

This later work by Howitt is carried out in pale reddish
brown, save for the grey-toned hills, towards which the
brown, dark in the foreground, gradually fades. The house
and the animals are delicately pencilled, but the rest of
the drawing is painted entirely with the brush. A comparison
with the previous illustration shows clearly the different
tree treatment used by Howitt in his later years.

115

34 THOMAS ROWLANDSON (1756–1827)

The Hazard Room [$13\frac{1}{8} \times 18\frac{3}{16}$ ins.]

Though Rowlandson was a master of landscape painting of
great beauty, he is better known for the grotesque caricatures
of humans which people his groves and villages, coastal and
river scenes, and his village inns. There is a type of
Rowlandson drawing, on the other hand, which depicts the
world of fashion of his day, its social figures and its
hangers-on, some of them only slightly caricatures, often
according to their degree. This example shows the artist's
very bold, swift and accurate brushwork over fine pencil,
and an accuracy of detail which had made his drawings so
valuable to the historian. Each of the gamblers is a master-
piece of characterisation, and Rowlandson's trick of drawing
the eye first to the pool of light in the centre is one that
has been imitated by at least one present-day cartoonist.

116

35 THOMAS ROWLANDSON (1756–1827)

A View of the Hague [11¼ × 16¾ ins.]

This townscape illustrates another aspect of Rowlandson's talents.
The architectural details are in every way correct, but were put
in with the same verve and economy which characterises Rowlandson's
caricatures. The drawing is also alive with people going about their
rather mundane day-to-day activities.

118

36 JOSEPH BARBER (1757–1811)
Landscape with Castle and Figures

[11⅝ × 16⅜ ins.]

David Cox had lessons at an
evening school kept by this
Birmingham artist, whose own
work was in the style of
William Payne. Little is known
about him, for apparently he
did not exhibit, though he had
a good local reputation for
his picturesque landscapes. This
is a typical example which
contains all Barber's usual
ingredients—the ruined castle,
the distant mountains, the low
cliff to the right, and the
group of figures.

37 WILLIAM BLAKE (1757–1827)

Self Portrait [7½ × 5¾ ins.]

William Blake was exactly contemporary with Rowlandson,
equally apart from others in the unique character of his
work, but possessing instead of Rowlandson's down-to-earth
cynicism the poetical spirit of a visionary who was not
understood by his fellow men. They looked on him as a madman.
From this self portrait, drawn in firm, flowing line, and
tinted, we may perhaps draw our own conclusions.

38 WILLIAM BLAKE (1757–1827)

St. Augustine and the British Captives [7¼ × 10¾ ins.]

This drawing does not feature the kind of mad terror or rage
which Blake was so well able to express in the faces of his
figures, but other characteristics of his work are clearly
to be seen. Thus, we have the strangely elongated figures,
some naked but others partly covered by clinging robes, the
smooth-muscled, small-handed arms, and every face with
a long, straight nose and receding forehead.

39 JOHN THOMAS SERRES (1759–1825)

Harbour Scene with Shipping [12½ × 17 ins.]

John Thomas was the eldest son of Dominic and succeeded his
father in 1793 as marine artist to the King, while at the
same time he was appointed marine draughtsman to the Admiralty.
His sea pieces, of which this drawing is typical, are drawn
with a firm and flowing pen and tinted in greys, blue-green
and yellow-green, often with splashes of brighter colour for
seamen's clothes. In this particular case the brighter yet
still soft colour is seen in the clothes of the seamen in
the foreground and in the flags. The general effect is one
of lightness and perfect calm.

40 DOMINIC M. SERRES (*fl.* 1778–1804)

Landscape with Bridge [12½ × 16½ ins.]: S. and D. 1790

D. M. Serres, son of Dominic Serres, R.A., exhibited landscapes
at the Academy between 1778 and 1804, but examples of his work
are quite rare. This drawing, being signed and dated, is
illustrated as being representative of his work as a landscape
water-colourist. It is tinted over pencil in tones of brown and grey.

124

41 WILLIAM PAYNE (*c.* 1760–1830)

A Creek with Boat and Figures

[8⅛ × 11⅜ ins.]: S.

Most of Payne's exhibited drawings
feature scenes in Devon
and Cornwall, though Welsh
subjects appear after 1809 and
Lake District ones after 1811.
Very occasionally, among the
many Payne drawings to be found,
the location of the place is
recognisable or, even more
rarely, indicated. Though some of
his early drawings show a Sandby
influence, being carefully
drawn, with trees outlined with
the pen, and prettily coloured,
his later and usual work is very
different. He had a particular
liking for orange-brown and
grey, and indeed invented the
pigment known as 'Payne's Grey'
which even nowadays is a
very useful water-colourist's
pigment. Though one does occasionally find a drawing with
blue in the sky and distant
mountains, the more usual effect,
due to fading, is one of
dark brown and orange. One of
Payne's tricks, the use of
dragging of the brush to give
texture in the foreground, is
clearly visible in this example.

42 WILLIAM GREEN (1760–1823)

A View in Westmorland [$16\frac{1}{2} \times 24\frac{3}{4}$ ins.]

Green was a Manchester man who, after a short stay in London,
returned north to paint views in the Lake District. This is
a most typical example of his work—mountains in the background, a lake and cows in the foreground. The drawing is
good, especially in the foreground, and the general colouring,
as usual, reddish brown and dull yellow. It has been suggested
that this rather monotonous colour scheme may be due to fading,
but I have seen examples preserved in portfolios which have
exactly the same appearance. The peculiar texture of the
hills is typical.

43 WILLIAM GREEN (1760–1823)

Windermere from Belmont Grove [14×19 ins.]

The similarities between the foreground treatments in this
and the previous drawing should be noticed, and also the
characteristic flecking of the foliage in the left foreground
tree. Though the colouring is dull green and reddish brown, the
effect is more sunlit and open than is usual in Green's work.

126

127

44 JOHN LAPORTE (1761–1839)

Landscape with Cart and Horses [$13\frac{1}{2}$ × $17\frac{7}{8}$ ins.]: S. and D.

This simple country landscape has a feature often found in Laporte's work, the tall trees on the left (which in other drawings may be replaced by a building or a cliff) lead down diagonally to the skyline to the point where the lane reverses the motion to return to the left foreground. Exactly the same treatment is to be seen in the *Italian Landscape* illustrated in Iolo Williams, save that the point of the triangle, as it were, is lower down the drawing. In addition, both are in body-colour which, in the case of our example, has the effect of giving a flattened, subdued appearance to the colouring, which is not visible in the photograph.

45 WILLIAM FREDERICK WELLS (1762–1836)

Rustic Scene [$10\frac{1}{2} \times 16\frac{1}{2}$ ins.]: S. and D. 1829

A very accomplished drawing, carefully pencilled and washed
in with bright, unfaded colours which are yet extremely soft.
As usual in Wells's best work, every wash is quite translucent.
The illustration shows the exquisite detail throughout. The
artist did not make use here of his usual long, narrow, dark
brush stroke in the foliage, nor of the clumping together
into one large leaf, as it were, of small leaf-sprays as he
did in a similar drawing in my possession which belonged to
the Wells family. Wells was a close friend of Turner and
one of the founders of the Old Water Colour Society.

I

130

46 THOMAS WALMSLEY
(1763–1805 or 6)
Mountainous Landscape

[7¾ × 11 ins.]: S. and D.

This body-colour drawing is
unusual because it is painted
entirely in blue, with the typical
almost white highlights.
Much of Walmsley's work, particularly his Welsh and Irish
scenes, was engraved, for which
purpose it was entirely
suitable because, as in a moon-
light subject in my possession,
he always shows a remarkable
understanding of tone values,
however limited his palette. The
characteristic tree treatment
is noteworthy, painted, as
indeed appears to be all his
work, without any pencilwork.
Most of Walmsley's drawings
are dramatic in character, and
he was indeed a scene
painter in Dublin and the
King's Theatre, Covent Garden.

47 JOHN WHITE ABBOTT
(1763–1851)
The Bonhay, Exeter

[13⅝ × 19¼ ins.]: Inse. and D.

John White Abbott was one of a
distinguished group of amateur artists.
He was born at Exeter and was a
pupil of Francis Towne. Although he
aspired to paint wholly in oils, and
did exhibit at the Royal Academy,
his talents were obviously in the
field of drawing. Abbott's water-
colours are basically drawings washed
over with rather flat colour.
His drawing is exceedingly accomplished as is his sense of pictorial
composition. Most of his work was
done in and around Devon, where he
lived the greater part of his life.

133

48 GEORGE BARRETT (1767–1842)

Warwick Castle [$14\frac{1}{2} \times 23\frac{1}{2}$ ins.]: S.

Few of George Barrett's drawings are not entirely pleasant
to live with, and since he was most prolific and invariably
competent, he has many admirers. Though in his early days he
exhibited views of the Thames Valley and Wales, he later
developed his romantic classical landscapes, such as this
typical example. The usual ingredients include an effect of
glowing light such as a sunrise or sunset, a lake or river,
some kind of classical building, a few figures in the foreground (often including a shepherd) and several animals. The
usual general tone of his work is brown.

134

49 GEORGE BARRETT (1767–1842)

The End of the Day [12¼ × 16½ ins.]

More purely a landscape than a poetical fantasy, this Barrett
is unusual also in that it has a blue sky, with the rays of
the early evening sun casting a yellow light from behind the
clouds upon the town in the distance. Barrett drew many similar
subjects with a human interest, with little groups of figures
in the foreground toiling homewards, resting by the wayside,
or simply standing, but invariably facing the setting sun.

50 JOSHUA CRISTALL (*c.* 1767–1847)

Study of a Sewing Girl [11¼ × 8⅞ ins.]

Joshua Cristall was hardly known to the general public before
1805, when he was a founder member of the Old Water Colour
Society, nor indeed was he ever able to profit financially
from his work. He was apparently a man of many parts, for in
his earlier years he was a china painter at Caughley in
Shropshire and, as was by no means uncommon at that time, an
occasional decorator of Stourbridge area glass. Though capable
of painting fine landscapes, he is nowadays known for his
sentimentally rustic subjects, such as the one chosen here.
His method of painting was to wash everything in upon a faint
pencil outline in very pale tones, after which every colour
was built up and strengthened, with shadows finally washed
in grey. His characteristic palette includes purplish brown,
mauve-pink, yellowish-green and greyish-blue.

51 JOHN GLOVER (1767–1849)

On the Wye [15½ × 23½ ins.]

Glover was born in Leicestershire, lived in London after the
Old Society exhibition of 1805, travelled in France, Switzerland and Italy, and in 1831 migrated to Tasmania, where he
died. He is known to collectors mainly by reason of his
trick of dividing the hairs of his brush into several points
which enabled him to paint the foliage of trees quickly.
This is not a typical Glover composition, but his use of the
split brush is clearly shown, as is his habit of flooding the
middle distance with light coming across the picture from one
side. The colours were applied over washes of Indian ink, and
because Barrett used indigo with Indian red for the sky, it is
as usual rather faded.

138

52 SAMUEL OWEN (*c.* 1768–1857)

Fishing Boats at Sea [10 × 16½ ins.]

In contrast to the following example of Owen's work, this is
typically early nineteenth century, still accurate as regards
the detail of boats and rigging, but meant to appeal to the
art lover rather than to the seaman. Again, we have the blue-
green sea flecked with white, the brown shipping and the
cobalt blue sky, applied over the careful ink drawing.

53 SAMUEL OWEN
(*c.* 1768–1857)

The Capture of La Minerve *by* **H.M.S.** Dido *and* Lowestoffe

24th June 1795 [13¾ × **19 ins.**]

On the back of this spirited marine drawing is pasted a contemporary newspaper account of the action which it depicts. The drawing is precisely formal and accurate in the manner of the eighteenth-century marine draughtsman, unlike most of Owen's work, which has a more picturesque approach. The ink drawing is meticulous, the sky cobalt blue tinged with grey, the ships brown, and the sea rich blue-green with white patches of foam. In contrast, the red and blue of the seamen's clothes, the tricolour and the red ensign are bright and unfaded.

54 THOMAS BARKER
(1769–1847)
Landscape with River
[$17\frac{3}{8} \times 25\frac{1}{2}$ ins.]

Thomas Barker or *Barker of Bath*
as he is usually called, was
with his brother Benjamin the
mainstay of the small Bath
school of water-colourists. The
rather woolly texture of his
work is shown here, as are the
scratched-out lights in the
water and the wiped-out highlights
in the foliage.

143

144

55 WILLIAM HENRY PYNE (1769–1843)
Fishermen's Houses by the Thames
[9¾ × 13¾ ins.]: S. and D. 1806

This is a late drawing by a founder of the Old
Society whose work is nevertheless rather
rare, and in the absence of a signature
difficult to attribute because he did not
confine himself to any one style. His subjects
are more often interiors, with figures in the
style of Morland or Rowlandson, but here
we have what is a quite different kind of study
almost in the manner of Girtin, with great
attention to detail and full of colour.

56 ROBERT HILLS (1769–1844)

A Stag Hunt [19½ × 27¼ ins.]: S. and D.

As an animal painter Hills is better known than almost any
other early nineteenth-century water-colourist, and
his deer are to be seen in many of his fine landscapes,
while he is known to have drawn the animals in landscapes by
other artists, particularly by G. F. Robson. He painted in
two distinct styles, at first in subdued tones (in a 'silvery'
manner, as Iolo Williams describes it) with foliage meticulously drawn, and later using hot, reddish colours with, in
my opinion, less attention to detail. In this drawing that
kind of colour is to be seen, but there is evidence in the
drawing of the hunted stag of his special ability.

146

57 ROBERT HILLS (1769–1844)

At Bailey's Hill, Kent [11¼ × 16 ins.]: S. and D.

Many of Hills's landscapes, at best spacious and clear of
atmosphere, typify what to most people is the fast-vanishing
pastoral England, and many of them feature Bailey's Hill and
the farm at the top end of this lane. Though comparatively
late, this drawing is in the artist's earlier style, full of
detail, softly coloured. It is probably the drawing that was
exhibited at the O.W.C.S. Exhibition in 1818, under the title
of *Road Scene near Bailey's Hill, Kent*.

148

58 WILLIAM DANIELL (1769–1837)

Durham Cathedral [15¾ × 25⅝ ins.]: S. and D. 1805

A fine example of Daniell's English drawings, dramatic, yet
at the same time peaceful and very much in the Girtin style.
Much of Daniell's work, first drawn delicately in soft pencil
as we see in the cathedral towers, is pretty rather than im-
pressive, but this is one of the drawings which in its rather
sombre majesty shows that the artist, not usually reckoned
as important, was capable of greatness.

149

59 FRANZ JOSEPH MANSKIRSCH (1770–1827)

Landscape with Castle [7⅜ × 9¼ ins.]

Manskirsch was a German who worked in this country between
about 1796 and 1805. Though he usually worked in pen or
pencil, or painted in monochrome, his rare drawings in full
colour, rather in the Girtin manner, show that he has been
underrated. This example, delicately coloured in blues and
blue-greens, is very similar in feeling to the *Village Church
by River* in the Whitworth Art Gallery.

150

60 JAMES BOURNE, R.A. (1773–1854)

Kelsey [11⅞ × 17 ins.]

James Bourne has the reputation of being a prolific but
rather dull artist. He travelled widely in Britain, and his
drawings are mostly topographical, but he was very partial
to compositions of the kind seen here, featuring cottages
in clumps of trees, in this case painted in brown monochrome,
as many of his drawings were. It shows a firmness of touch
and a clarity of outline not usually associated with his work.

61 JAMES BOURNE, R.A.

Cottage near Dolgelly

[11⅝ × 16⅞ ins.]

A very typical, restful drawing in Bourne's rather romanticised topographical style, with his usual cottage among the trees. His foliage treatment is unmistakable, as is his rather woolly style and his subdued yet rich colouring in greys, grey-greens, pale orange-yellow, and touches of brighter red and blue for the figures.

153

62 HUGH WILLIAM 'GRECIAN' WILLIAMS (1773–1829)

Inverary [15⅛ × 20½ ins.]: D. 1806

Hugh Williams at first painted this kind of Scottish landscape, but his reputation was made as the result of a tour
of Italy and Greece, from which he returned in 1818. He
published an account of his travels with engravings after
his own drawings, exhibited many water-colours of Greece, and
was thereafter known by his nickname. This drawing is in a
pleasing colour scheme of blue-green, dull green and fawn-
brown, with the figures outlined in brown with the brush.

63 RICHARD SASSE (1774–1849)

Limerick [18⅛ × 26 ins.]: S.

The original spelling of this artist's name was Sass. He was
appointed teacher of drawing to Princess Charlotte in 1811,
and afterwards landscape painter to the Prince Regent. Much
of his work is nondescript, but an occasional drawing such as
this example and a fine Lancaster in the Victoria and Albert
Museum show him to have been an artist of great ability. The
colours are subdued save for the gay reds and blues of the
figures in the foreground. On the back of the drawing, in the
artist's hand, the full title is written—*Ruins of Askiaten,
Nr. Limerick, Ireland, Richard Sass, 1810.*

155

64 GEORGE CHINNERY (1774–1852)

Boat Dwellings, Macao, China [$3\frac{1}{2} \times 5\frac{1}{4}$ ins.]

After working in Dublin for a few years Chinnery went to India, and in 1825 moved to China, where he lived until his death. He was apparently more interested in recording the life of the people in the form of sketches rather than as finished water-colours. This is a small drawing, but satisfyingly rich in colour and fluent in line.

65 PAUL SANDBY MUNN (1775–1845)

A Castle Gateway [$11\frac{7}{8}$ × 18 ins.]

Munn was Paul Sandby's godson, and is said to have had his
first lessons from that great man. He was a friend of Cotman,
from whom he inherited something of a sense of colour and
design that may sometimes be seen in his work, though like
William Turner of Oxford he never fulfilled his early promise.
In this drawing, which is reminiscent of the style of Cornelius
Varley, he shows his preference for a restricted area,
and for soft, restrained colours. It shows a strength of
touch which indicates a fairly early date, for his later work
was inclined to be woolly and rather flat.

66 WILLIAM DELAMOTTE (1775–1863)

The Jetty at Dieppe [5⅝ × 9¼ ins.]: S.

Delamotte was born at Weymouth
in the same year as Turner
and Girtin, and some of his
work is reminiscent of theirs.
He painted views in England,
Wales and on the Continent,
usually of the picturesque kind,
using a firm reddish-brown
ink or pencil outline, as in
this example, which has a blue
sky shading to faint purple on
the horizon, with the rest
washed in with grey and reddish brown.

159

160

67 THOMAS GIRTIN (1775–1802)

Ripon Cathedral [$10\frac{1}{8}$ × $16\frac{7}{8}$ ins.]

Thomas Girtin was short-lived, and little is known about his
life. Nevertheless, he shares with his friend Turner a place
extremely high in English water-colour art. As a topographer
he was perhaps best in architectural subjects, capable of
rendering buildings in beautiful washes of greyish-brown and
blue richly and freely, while his landscapes, like those of
De Wint, express on a few square inches of paper the whole
breadth of the world. This small drawing is softly subdued,
with no hard outlines and no visible pencil work.

This typical piece of architectural topography is subdued in
colour, beautifully pencilled and freely handled. Notice the
effective placing of the dark tree masses and the introduction
of the almost white bridge and house into what is otherwise
a drawing carried out in greys, browns and dull green.

161

68 and 69 JOSEPH MALLORD WILLIAM TURNER (1775–1851)

Calais Pier, the arrival of the English Packet [13⅞ × 19½ ins.]

The subject of this drawing was chosen by many artists, but
the sheer grandeur of this exquisite work is outstanding. It
is indeed a water-colour version of the oil painting in the
National Gallery, and was reproduced as a coloured aquatint
in 1921 by G. J. Howell & Co. The amazing detail apart—for
this is only perceived after the eye is sated with the overall
strength of the drawing—the drama of the violent sea and the
puny humans battling against it is vividly captured. The clear
spaces of the sky are cobalt blue, the storm-clouds intense
blue green, the sea a beautiful translucent green and the
figures brightly coloured. The subject on the left, *Flounder Fishing
near Putney*, is unusually placid for Turner and shows a little
known side of his prodigious output. It contrasts
strongly with the vital movement of *Calais Pier* below.

70 JOSEPH MALLORD WILLIAM TURNER (1775–1851)

Ivy Bridge [11 × 15½ ins.]

In quite a different style, but painted in similar colours
to those in the previous illustration, this drawing is done
with great sureness and delicacy, while the whole has an
undefinable, smooth appearance. Notice the several little
points of carefully drawn interest—the coach and the figures
on the bridge, the ducks, and the basket and bundle in the
right foreground. There is an almost exactly similar drawing
in the National Gallery.

71 JOHN CONSTABLE (1776–1837)

Landscape with Castle [15$\frac{7}{8}$ × 20$\frac{1}{8}$ ins.]: S.

Constable was, of course, primarily an oil painter, and his work in water-colour was for the most part incidental. This drawing is in pen, pencil and black chalk, but even so, it is an example of the amazing atmospheric effects of which Constable was master, and of the spontaneity with which he handled even his larger drawings.

72 BENJAMIN BARKER (1776–1838)

Brecon Town and Bridge

[15¾ × 23 ins.]: S.

An unusually powerful
drawing by one of
the two brothers who
founded the Bath
School of water-colour
drawing. It is topo-
graphical, and not
so woolly as are most
of his brother's
drawings, effectively
contrasting the dark
mass of the bridge
with the lighter
colour beyond.

167

73 JOHN THIRTLE (1777–1839)

Landscape with Figures [7 × 10 ins.]

Thirtle exhibited with the Norwich Society from 1805, and until recently his fame was almost entirely local. Much of his work is reminiscent of Cotman, whose wife's sister he married, in its arrangement of spaces of light and dark, in pure washes of colour, but on the whole his pleasant, almost feminine sketches are more attractive. This example is delicately handled, the colours subdued and the sense of space and distance well achieved.

74 JOHN VARLEY (1778–1842)

Hampstead Heath [9¼ × 12 ins.]: S. and D. 1826

At this period of Varley's life he often painted scenes of
this kind, as being perhaps of greater appeal to the general
public. Another Hampstead view *Frognal* is in the Victoria and
Albert Museum. In this example, however, he did not descend
to the prettiness, the too great detail of drawing which is
sometimes seen in this kind of later work. The trees are
drawn in an almost cursory manner reminiscent of the 'compositions' Varley drew to teach his pupils.

169

170

75 JOHN VARLEY (1778–1842)

The Eagle's Nest, Killarney

[11½ × 14 ins.]: S.

John Varley is without doubt
one of the best known water-
colourists to the general public,
certainly one of the most
attractive, and perhaps one of
the most versatile.
We know that Varley was wont to
paint landscapes of scenes
he never visited, using his
typical formula, and I believe
this drawing to be a case in
point. Whereas so many of his
water-colours lack interest in
the sky (often due to fading)
we have here a beautiful cloud-
scape. Also clearly visible is
Varley's characteristic treatment
of still water with broad,
horizontal strokes of a full brush.

76 JOHN VARLEY (1778–1842)

The Monnow Bridge, Monmouth [4 × 7 ins.]

Varley's drawings of the Hereford, Shrewsbury and Leominster areas may be dated between *c.* 1799 and 1802, and were presumably made during his early Welsh tours. This small example, exquisitely pencilled and tinted in subdued browns, pale reds and fawns, shows not only Varley's fine draughtsmanship but also his sense of texture, eye for perspective and understanding of antiquity. Notice the choice of the arch, from which the eye is drawn to every other point of interest in the composition, and the fine drawing of the figures.

172

77 LUKE CLENNELL (1781–1840)

Kirkstall Abbey [16¼ × 20¾ ins.]

Luke Clennell was apprenticed to Thomas Bewick, the wood-engraver, and is well known for his engravings of pen-and-ink drawings by Stothard. In 1810 he gave up engraving and turned to water-colour, becoming an Associate of the O.W.C.S. in 1812, and drawing figure groups of contemporary life. In many of these he shows a strong sense of the dramatic, which is, however, better expressed in his rare landscapes. The abbey is strongly outlined in brown ink over yellow and brown washes, and body-colour is used for the sky and for the trail of smoke. Clennell was probably so impressed by the majesty of his subject that he chose this close-up view, although a more distant one might have made a better composition.

78 CORNELIUS VARLEY
(1781–1873)

A Fishing Village [7¾ × 9⅞ ins.]

Though admittedly Cornelius was neither so prolific nor so technically skilful as his brother John, he was nevertheless his equal in the use of pure colour, usually in the subdued browns, fawns and greys with which this pencilled drawing is tinted. Cornelius knew how to paint a peaceful, harmonious water-colour, making effective use of patches of light and shade, and at his best there is good excuse for attributing his work to his more famous brother.

174

79 JOHN SELL COTMAN (1782–1842)

A Windmill in Lincolnshire [19 × 15½ ins.]

Because Cotman was for some time working under Dr. Monro, who
in turn had taught (and doubtless learned much from) Girtin,
his early work was influenced by that master's style. Later
on, after about 1805, he evolved the style for which he is
so well known, the clear-cut patterning of washes of contrasting, pure colours that is comparable only with the work
of Francis Towne. At the same time the many changes in his
style were such that generalisation is impossible, and his
work must be studied in detail. Apart from any other influencing
factor, like many water-colourists Cotman worked indoors
upon outdoor pencil drawings, with the result that, for
instance, there are four versions of the example illustrated here.

80 JOHN SELL COTMAN (1782–1842)

An Indian Temple [12½ × 18¼ ins.]

Cotman never visited India, and this drawing must be either
an imaginary composition or have been taken, possibly, from
an engraving. It is probably rather late. In it, the artist
has made full use of the contrasting vivid blue of the sky
and the pale golden domes of the temple, of the white cloud
and the dark brown, almost black oxen and their driver.

81 WILLIAM HAVELL (1782–1857)

River Scene with Fishermen [17⅜ × 23⅜ ins.]

William Havell worked with David Cox at Hastings in 1812, and had been able to watch John and Cornelius Varley and Joshua Cristall. It would be strange therefore if he had learned nothing from them, and in fact some of his work is extremely fine. He painted much in Wales and in the Lake District, published *A Series of Picturesque Views of the River Thames*, and visited China (as artist to Lord Amherst's Embassy) and Italy. He was at his best in painting sunlight effects, and his massing of cliff forms and treatment of trees in full foliage, as in this example, is second to none.

82 WILLIAM HAVELL (1782–1857)

Newport Castle, Monmouthshire [15¾ × 22⅛ ins.]

This is a serene and tranquil drawing, and as in so many of
Havell's water-colours, one feels that time stands still. It is
one of the sunlit scenes which Havell did so well, tinted in
grey, blue-green and yellow, the figures brighter in blue
and red. The treatment of the water is particularly fine,
with effective use of 'scratching out' with a knife.

179

83 SAMUEL PROUT (1783–1852)

A Fisherman's Hut

[15½ × 21 ins.]: S.

Prout's early work was confined
to English topography and
coastal scenes before he visited
the Continent in 1818 or
1819, after which he devoted
himself to the architectural
subjects for which he is well
known. This example of his
earlier work is tinted in the
browns, fawns and greys which
always remained typical of his
work, with brighter colour
for the group in the foreground,
and it is interesting to
see that in the treatment of
the woodwork of the hut there
are traces of the broken line
which later Prout used to such
effect on his stonework.

84 SAMUEL PROUT

Old House at Pound's Bridge, near Tonbridge

[12 × 17½ ins.]

In 1801, when Prout was only seventeen, the architectural antiquary John Britton was so impressed by his drawing that he invited the young artist to go with him to Cornwall in order to make sketches for his *Beauties of England and Wales*. The trip was not a success, for Prout apparently was quite unskilled in perspective, and in writing to thank his patron he said, 'I am at present very busy learning perspective. When better qualified to draw buildings, I will visit Launceston, Tavistock, etc. . . .' We now know that he succeeded, and that even during his preoccupation with the old buildings of Continental towns was still able to find time to draw the architecture of his own country.

85 SAMUEL PROUT (1783–1852)

Vincenza, Italy [18½ × 6½ ins.]

The many fine visits which Prout made to the Continent inspired
the fine drawing of crumbling masonry of which he is the acknow-
ledged master. As a draughtsman Prout has few equals, but in
addition he brought to his task a sympathy and a reverence for
old buildings that gave a subtle interest to his drawings that
is so often lacking in architectural subjects. Prout drew his
subject carefully in pencil, tinted it with his characteristic
fawns, browns and greys, with brighter patches of colour for
his figures and crowds, and finally outlined the stonework
with a reed pen. 'The reed pen outline and peculiar touch of
Prout are the only means of expressing the crumbling character of stone,' said Ruskin, by which he meant the irregular,
wavering outline which we refer to as the 'broken line'. This
fine example was drawn when Prout was sketching with J. D.
Harding for *Views of Cities and Scenery in Italy, France
and Switzerland* by Thomas Roscoe, published in 1836.

86 DAVID COX (1783–1859)

The Llug Meadows near Hereford [17½ × 30 ins.]

Late in 1814 David Cox went to Hereford as drawing-master in
Miss Croucher's seminary for young ladies at a salary of £100
a year. During his stay there, until he bought a house in
Kensington, in 1827, he made many drawings of local houses,
cottages and streets, and also produced a number of highly
finished pastoral scenes of the kind illustrated here. We
must suppose that they would find a ready sale as fashionable
drawing-room decorations, and doubtless eked out Cox's
miserable salary. Technically its smooth brush-work and
beautifully clear colour is faultless, however far removed
from the nervous, rougher, atmospheric work of his later years.

87 DAVID COX (1783–1859)

Farmyard at Bettws-y-Coed [$8\frac{1}{2}$ × $10\frac{1}{2}$ ins.]: S. and D. 1843

Wales had an ever-increasing fascination for Cox, because it
satisfied his urge, after about 1830, to paint the elemental
effects of weather and wild scenery rather than merely pretty
scenery. As a young man he stayed at the Swan Inn and later,
about 1845, at the Royal Oak, but according to local knowledge
he often lodged at the farmhouse which is the subject of this
illustration. Technically it is an unusually delicate drawing
for its date, showing typical Cox cattle and the figures which
always seem to have their back to the viewer.

186

88 DAVID COX (1783–1859)

Beaumaris, Anglesey [8½ × 12 ins.]: S. and D. 1847

As a marine painter Cox was equally at home with the lighter
tones and clear atmosphere of his famous *Rhyl Sands* and the
dark, lowering skies and violent seas of such a drawing as
that illustrated here. A feature of so many Cox stormy skies
is the presence of a lighter patch, as if to herald the end
of the tumult. We see it in one of his finest drawings *The
Challenge* (V. & A. Museum) and we see it here, with the sun
shining upon the distant town. This drawing was engraved in
Thomas Roscoe's *Windings and Execursions in North Wales.*

90 PETER DE WINT (1784–1849)

View from Gore Lane, Kensington, showing
St. Luke's Church, Chelsea [18⅝ × 8¼ ins.]

De Wint's landscapes are entirely typical of the English
scene, and one thinks of him in connection with riverside
meadows and pastoral scenes, though in fact he was also an
accomplished water-colourist of still life. In his landscapes
he was fond of the kind of shallow, wide panorama which is
illustrated here. It is not highly finished, and its attraction
lies in the typical long, shallow areas of contrasting
light and shade of sky, town and foreground.

89 DAVID COX (1783–1859)

The Churchyard at Bettws-y-Coed [15⅝ × 14¾ ins.]: S. and D.

About 1850 increasing eyesight weakness began to affect Cox's
work, with the result that though he continued to travel and
to work (despite a stroke suffered during the year this drawing was painted), his handling became rougher and he concentrated
more and more on atmospheric effects which did not require so
much attention to detail. Strangely enough (or, perhaps, is
it so strange considering their power?), it is this kind of
drawing, often of dreary, rainswept moorland or glen, which
is so sought-after. This example should be compared with the
Welsh Funeral, in oil, in the Birmingham Art Gallery; it was
drawn from the same viewpoint, but a little to the left. It
shows the full power of Cox's last period, the luminous blue
mountainside, the dark green, almost black trees, and the
slashing, incisive indications of the figures. There is
hardly any detail, but as Cox replied to those who criticised,
'Do they not forget these paintings are the work of the mind?'

189

92 PETER DE WINT (1784–1849)

Beverley Minster [$3\frac{5}{8} \times 6\frac{3}{8}$ ins.]

Though in such drawings as those of
buildings in Lincoln, De Wint used
a wealth of careful detail, he was
above all a master of the pure wash
of colour, laid on with a full brush,
into which, while still wet, he
flooded a mosaic of added tints, rich
and harmonious. He was able to do
this even in a drawing of this size,
again panoramic in shape. He was wont
to neglect his skies, preferring the
meadows beneath, but here the unfaded,
troubled greys and blues are a perfect
backcloth against which the white
tower stands out sharply. The clumps
of trees are arbitrary, with no care
for species, a common feature of
De Wint's work.

91 PETER DE WINT (1784–1849)

Gloucester Cathedral [7 × 12 ins.]

Gloucester Cathedral was apparently
a favourite De Wint subject, and this
drawing may be compared with the
Gloucester, 1840, in the V. & A. Museum,
illustrated in *Water-colour Painting
in Britain* by Martin Hardie, Plate
201. The foreground tree in particular
is an object lesson in De Wint's
use of wash, as is the foreground, in
dull greys and browns which are yet
vividly rich in glowing colour. The
sky is grey with a little red washed
in, and red is repeated in the roofs
of the houses.

93 WILLIAM FLEETWOOD
VARLEY (1785–1856)

View near Gravesend [$7\frac{3}{4} \times 10\frac{3}{8}$ ins.]

Although this drawing is rather
pretty, and much more colourful than those of his brothers
John and Cornelius, there is
a kinship in his use of washes,
though he did not use John's
wet-brush, wide strokes in the
water. At times this younger
brother was capable of making
drawings that could well be
mistaken for those of his elders,
but owing to being nearly
burnt to death, he seems to
have done no work after about 1820.

94 ANTHONY VANDYKE COPLEY FIELDING (1787–1855)

Bolton Abbey from the Wharfe [11 × 18¼ ins.]: S. and D. 1810

Copley Fielding was elected an Associate of the O.W.C.S. in
1810, and included in the 1811 Exhibition was a number of
drawings which were the result of a tour through the Lake
District to Scotland which he had made. As indicated by the
date, this drawing was probably made at that time. The sky
treatment is beautifully done, and the whole colour scheme
subdued in a style which he later forsook in a search for
something more striking. In quite another style, also, Copley
Fielding was able very closely to imitate Varley in his use
of simple line, carefully placed mass and strongly colour washes.

194

95 ANTHONY VANDYKE COPLEY FIELDING (1787–1855)

Coastal Scene [7 × 10¼ ins.]

After 1816, as the result of spending some time on the South
Coast, Copley Fielding began to paint seascapes, more often
of stormy seas against lowering skies. These he produced by
wash upon wash of thin colour, laboriously, to obtain good
atmospheric effects, in which the colours of the sea and sky
are always completely in harmony. In this example there is
an effective gradation from the grey and blue sky to the
green sea, down to the brown beach.

195

96 GEORGE FENNELL ROBSON (1788–1833)

Loch Katrine [8¾ × 15 ins.]

A long visit to Scotland about 1810 gave Robson a taste for highland scenery, and thereafter most of his exhibited drawings were of Scottish views. Though at times he was capable of highly dramatic effects (as we see in his *Loch Coruisk, Isle of Skye*, in the V. & A. Museum, and illustrated by

Hardie, Vol. II, Pl. 215), his water-colours were praised by
his contemporaries for their 'depth of repose', and it is that
quality, attained by a subdued, overall brown and yellow-green
appearance, a peculiar, almost misty texture and a serenity
which appeals so much to modern collectors. In this example
the key to this serenity is supplied by the lovely, placid
surface of the lake.

97 PETER LA CAVE (*c.* 1789–1816)

Landscape with Windmill

[$9\frac{7}{8} \times 15$ ins.]

This French water-colourist is said to have worked in England from about 1789 to 1816, and so is conveniently included in this section, though he was obviously born at an earlier date. He usually worked to a formula of a ford or drinking place, a horse and rider, or a cart, and a few cattle, and several rustic figures, outlined in pen and prettily coloured. This done, trees and other surroundings were washed in rather carelessly, apparently without any preliminary drawing, in general tones of blue-greens and grey.

199

98 PETER LA CAVE (*c*. 1789–1816)

A Village Encounter [9 × 13¼ ins.]

This is one of Le Cave's more thoughtful drawings, free and
pleasant, with each figure and animal well and carefully outlined with a pen, and the whole tinted in blue-greys and yellows.

99 WILLIAM HENRY HUNT (1790–1864)

The Fortune Tellers [29 × 20½ ins.]: S.

Hunt was apprentice to John Varley before becoming a student
of the Royal Academy in 1808. He at first painted in oils,
but devoted himself entirely to water-colours after being
elected a full member of the *Old Society* in 1826. His first
love as a water-colourist was the painting of homely, humorous
rustic figures, especially children, though later he painted
fruit and flowers with great skill, usually accompanied
by a bird's nest, so that he is often known as 'Bird's Nest
Hunt'. The example I illustrate here is painted mainly in
body-colour, the faces and hands delicately stippled in the
greatest detail, and the clothing filled in with short strokes
of the brush to give almost a stippled effect on these larger
surfaces. There is a great deal of knife work to give texture
to the clothing, and the colouring throughout is bright, solid
and sure. Above all, the characterisation of the children's
faces, their looks of dismay and elfishness, is masterly.

202

100 JOHN LINNELL (1792–1882)
Hayfield with Approaching Storm
[7 × 8⅞ ins.]

Linnell was a pupil of Varley, with Turner of Oxford, W. H. Hunt and David Cox. Though he concentrated on oil painting after about 1820 he never entirely gave up water-colours, and always had a particular liking for ripened cornfields beneath cumulus cloud. There is a little of Cox in this example, if we take away the children, and as a change from what Samuel Palmer called 'those glorious round clouds which you paint' the sky here is dark and threatening.

101 CLARKSON STANFIELD, R.A. (1793–1867)

Blackhorn Fort, Portsmouth [8¾ × 12⅛ ins.]: S. and D.

The name of William is often given in error to this artist, who served in the merchant service and in the Navy, whence after a fall he was discharged in 1818, to become a scene-painter at the Royalty Theatre in Wapping. Though during tours on the Continent in 1829 and 1839 he painted water-colour drawings in the style of Bonington and James Holland, he is best known for his marine subjects, into which he put all the knowledge and observation resulting from his years at sea. In this example there is a true conformity between sea and sky which is seen in all his drawings, and the be-haviour of the boats in a choppy sea is faithfully recorded.

102 CLARKSON STANFIELD, R.A. (1793–1867)

Sheerness, 1840 [7 × 10¼ ins.]

In contrast to the previous example of Stanfield's work, we can see here one of his drawings of the sea in peaceful mood. No artist has been better able to paint still water, and here again any lover of sailing will be able to see that his sails and rigging are faithfully drawn.

103 SAMUEL AUSTIN (1796–1834)

Continental Landscape [11⅝ × 18¼ ins.]

Samuel Austin was one of De Wint's less wealthy pupils—it
is recorded that someone paid for him to have three lessons
from the great man, and certainly in that short time Austin
learnt enough to enable him to paint very much in the De
Wint style. The example illustrated is an unusually important
piece of work, but on a smaller scale some of the artist's
studies of boats and figures are very charming, carefully
drawn and washed in with pure colour.

**104 JAMES DUFFIELD
HARDING [1797–1863)**

An Approaching Storm

[18¼ × 24¾ ins.]: S.

J. D. Harding had
lessons from Samuel
Prout, and though
he has been
shamefully neglected by
collectors and writers
alike, he painted
so well that on
more than one
occasion drawings
attributed to
Bonington have finally
been re-attributed to
him. Certainly at
best his Continental
street scenes, usually
crowded with well-drawn
figures, show an
understanding of
old architecture which
almost equals that
of Prout, while on
the other hand,
though many of his
smaller landscapes are
prettily coloured, he
could on occasion
produce the kind of
dramatic effect seen
in this example.
Unfortunately, it
loses much in
black and white, the
contrasting brown of
the middle distance
and the indigo of
the sky, and the
bright ultra-marine
flash of the stream.
As in most of
Harding's work, much
has been made of
Chinese white.

208

105 JAMES HOLLAND (*c.* 1800–70)

The Rialto at Venice [9 × 15⅜ ins.]

Like Cristall, Holland seems to have begun his career as a
pottery painter; he was born in Burslem, the son of a potter.
From the Potteries he went to London, where he painted flowers,
but he is best known for his paintings of the lagoons and canals
of Venice, very much in the style of Bonington. This is a late
drawing, done in 1865, and noteworthy for its beautiful detail,
fine composition and brilliant colour.

106 JAMES HOLLAND (*c.* 1800–70)

Forest Scene [11¾ × 17 ins.]: S. and D. 1851

Had this powerful drawing not been signed, would it have been correctly attributed? The colours, though strong, with the highlights done in Chinese white, are not so hot as we see in Holland's Venetian drawings.

212

107 GEORGE CATTERMOLE (1800–68)

Macbeth giving instructions to the Murderers [11½ × 15½ ins.]: S.

A similar example of Cattermole's work is in the Whitworth
Art Gallery, and another in the Victoria and Albert Museum
[see *Water Colour Paintings*, pub. by the Museum, 1927].
Though Cattermole set out to be an architectural painter,
his reputation today is that of a figure painter, wholly
with an historical or literary connection, and for the most
part essentially dramatic. He was one of the first English
artists, in fact, who set out to record historic times with
complete accuracy, to which purpose he made a deep study of
the buildings, furnishings and costume of medieval years.
In keeping with the subject, this example is painted
predominantly in reds of varying tones.

213

214

108 GEORGE CATTERMOLE (1800–68)

Cattle Raid at Gilnockie Tower
[11¾ × 16¾ ins.]

It is not generally known that Cattermole was an accomplished landscape painter, as may be seen in this example, though at the same time its subject is pseudo-historical. It is painted entirely in browns and greys, the brushwork characteristically spontaneous and dashing, and was reproduced in Lawson's *Scotland, Picturesque: Historical: Descriptive.*

215

109 JAMES BAKER PYNE
(1800–70)
Landscape in Palestine
[20 × 31 ins.]

It has been observed more than once that J. B. Pyne was an artist whose atmospheric effects show signs of an effort to follow Turner, and in fact this drawing, which is one of a pair, was for some time attributed to the latter. It is of extremely fine quality, the brushwork masterly, and gives a striking effect of blazing sunshine. Like many of Pyne's large drawings, the paper is pasted on to a canvas.

216

110 JAMES BAKER PYNE (1800–70)

Mountainous Landscape with Waterfall [$11\frac{1}{2} \times 16$ ins.]

In his day Pyne was known as a landscape painter, and in contrast to the Palestine drawing, this example of his work in that
regard has the dramatic force of the previous one. Skilful use
of the colour and texture of the paper is an essential in water-
colour painting, and here it is fully exemplified in the sky,
the mist between the mountains and the waterfall.

111 JAMES BAKER PYNE (1800–70)

The Boatyard [14½ × 19¾ ins.]: S.

There is evidence, again, in this dramatic drawing, of
Turner's influence on Pyne's work. Atmospheric effect,
certainly, in the general sombre tones, relieved by the
thrusting near-white of the prow and the intense red and
yellow flame of the fire. The drawing is meticulous. There
can be no doubt that Pyne is as yet greatly underrated,
though in his day his reputation was such that he taught
W. J. Miller and G. A. Fripp.

112 and 113 FRANCIS OLIVER FINCH (1802–62)

An Alpine Bridge [left] [10⅞ × 15½ ins.]: S.

Classical Composition [right] [9 × 11 ins.]

The drawings of Finch are often mistaken for George Barrett's,
particularly when they are of the same classical type and
have the same brownish colouring. He was a pupil of John
Varley, and his landscapes are usually 'compositions' (to use
Varley's expression) in the classical tradition.

220

114 FREDERICK TAYLER
(1802–89)

Harvest Time [9 × 12¾ ins.]

Beyond the fact that Tayler succeeded J. F. Lewis as President of the *Old Society*, and that he studied for some time with R. P. Bonington in Paris, little has been written about him and his work, although he was highly praised by Ruskin in his *Modern Painters* for his powerful sketching. Powerful, and at the same time nervous, is indeed well descriptive of his pencil and brush work in the usual rustic and sporting types of drawings which he did so well. This example, as usual, is freely, incisively drawn, and painted in full colour, with touches of Chinese white.

115 FREDERICK TAYLER (1802–89)

A Country Larder [15 × 18½ ins.]

This is an unusual subject for Tayler, but executed with his
typical facile handling, incisive touch and bright freshness.

116 RICHARD PARKES BONINGTON (1802–28)

French Coast with Fishing Boats [6¾ × 11¾ ins.]

Bonington moved to France with his parents in 1817 or 1818, and
remained there until his death. They lived in Calais, and the
boy's interest in sketching was seen by Francia, who taught
him how to paint in water-colour, after which he studied at
the Ecole des Beaux Arts in Paris and also worked in the
studio of Baron Gros. He paid three visits to England, and
also visited Italy. His work may be broadly divided into
three classes, picturesque architecture (he was in touch
with Prout), figure compositions, and coastal and river
scenes. He was a master of the 'broken wash', which allows
the tint of the paper, or an initial ground colour, to show
through in tiny gaps.

117 WILLIAM AND JOHN CANTILOE JOY
(Born 1803 and 1806, died 1867 and 1866)
Shipping on a Breezy Day [$8\frac{1}{2}$ × $11\frac{1}{2}$ ins.]
Among water-colourists who painted nothing but sea-scapes at
the beginning of the century were the brothers Joy of Yarmouth,
who worked for the most part in collaboration.

118 and 119 WILLIAM LEIGHTON LEITCH (1804–83)

Dumbarton from the River Leven [10⅜ × 16½ ins.]: S.

Leitch was born in Glasgow, was a scene painter at the
theatre there for some time and later, having moved to
London, he became a well-known teacher, giving instruction
to Queen Victoria for many years. His drawings are notable
for their careful finish, often very much like those of
David Roberts (who in fact helped him to obtain employment
as a scene painter in London). His colours are bright yet warmly
subdued. This example is an extremely fine one, drawn with
amazing detail, topographical, but full of busy interest.

Leith Hill from Reigate Common [14 × 22½ ins.]: S. and D.
This late drawing is a typical example of the landscape drawing of the time, accurately done and naturally coloured.

120 SAMUEL PALMER (1805–81)

Tintern Abbey

Samuel Palmer was something of a phenomenon in British art, a mystic who, inspired by William Blake, saw in the ordinary English countryside an ethereal beauty which he was able to incorporate, in glorious colour, in his drawings. Many water-colourists have painted Tintern Abbey, but none have so suc-ceeded in combining such exquisite detail with such an air of almost enchanted mystery. The foreground is left unfinished, which to me has the effect of repeatedly taking the eye back to the focal point of the drawing—the beautiful, delicately traced window. A beautiful example of Palmer's 'Shoreham' period work is reproduced on the cover of this book.

121 GEORGE CHAMBERS (1803–1840)

Dutch Boats in a Gale [$9\frac{3}{8} \times 14\frac{1}{8}$ ins.]: S.

George Chambers was the son of a fisherman and born at Whitby. At the age of eight he went to sea, but returned to Whitby at seventeen to be a house and ship painter. Several years later he returned to London, where he did various painting jobs, including being a scene painter at the Pavilion Theatre. His water-colours, as this example clearly shows, displayed a rare bravura style and one which was informed by a practical understanding of boats and the vicissitudes of the sea. His early death robbed us of one of the most outstanding marine painters of his time—indeed of any time.

227

122 JOHN SKINNER PROUT (1806–76)

German Village Scene [8 × 10¼ ins.]: S.

Skinner Prout, as he is usually called, was Samuel's nephew
and a sketching friend of W. J. Müller in Bristol, while
Skinner was preparing his *Antiquities of Bristol*. Some of
his drawings are very similar to those of his uncle, particularly his Bristol ones, but usually, as in this example, his
drawing is freer, often much resembling that of William Callow,
and his colouring altogether brighter.

123 CHARLES BENTLEY (1806–54)

Trebizond [15½ × 22½ ins.]

No marine water-colourist has excelled Bentley in his rendering of salt water, which is almost invariably translucent,
with a wonderful greenish tinge and depth. He confined himself almost wholly to coastal scenes, and particularly
pleasant are his small studies of rocky beaches, with here
and there a rocky pool or a fisherman's boat, washed in over
faint pencil outline, but with the details of rocks, fishermen's clothes, etc., outlined with the point of the brush.

125 THOMAS COLMAN DIBDIN (1810–93)
After the Storm [13½ × 20 ins.]: S. and D. 1836
Dibdin is better known as a painter of architectural subjects,
and particularly of French towns and cathedrals, but this
example of his work in a completely different vein presents
him as a marine painter with a keen sense of the dramatic.

124 LOUIS HAGHE (1806–85)
A Cathedral Interior [24¾ × 18¾ ins.]: S.
Haghe's interest was always torn between figure drawing and
the faithful rendering of medieval architecture, in particular
that of France and Belgium. He was the son of an architect,
and having lost the use of his right hand from birth, he
painted entirely with his left. He may be compared with
Cattermole as regards choice and type of subject, but his
work is much more careful, and invariably contains a great
deal of body-colour, with much ruler work and precise drawing
of small detail. The example illustrated is remarkable of its
kind, not only for its size. In full colour, the effect of
the light shining from the top right-hand corner faithfully
observed and rendered, the perspective immaculate, the various
shining marbles too heavy to lift by reason of their apparent
solidity and the well-drawn figures judiciously and naturally
positioned, of its kind it is Haghe at his considerable best.

231

126 WILLIAM CALLOW (1812–1908)

Old Houses at Berncastel on the Moselle [14½ × 19 ins.]: S. and D.

In 1829 Callow went to Paris where he met Thomas Shotter Boys and was encouraged by him to paint street scenes. Before about 1850 was his best period, distinguished by bold line without a great deal of detail, an effective massing of light and shade, and a fine sense of colour. These features, except the last, can be seen in this example, as can be Callow's characteristic way of drawing figures.

127 WILLIAM CALLOW (1812–1908)

Tynemouth [11¼ × 16½ ins.]: S.

Callow painted both in water-colour and in oils, and while his many coastal scenes are more successful in the latter medium, the example illustrated is typical of his drawings, with a very good sky, a large vessel silhouetted against it, rocks and seaweed in the foreground, and a few figures. Callow, at first at any rate, was a traditionalist in his art. That is to say, over a precise drawing he applied his washes, building them up over a non-absorbent paper adding detail with the point of the brush, using no tricks of rubbing and scraping, and very rarely using body-colour.

128 WILLIAM CALLOW (1812–1908)
A Rustic Scene with Bridge [10 × 13¼ ins.]: S. and D. 1875
This drawing is not oval because of its mount, but was painted
in that form, a common practice of Callow in his later period
when he produced drawings of this kind for his own pleasure,
of no particular place. Some are mere sketches, lightly washed
with colour, and others, like this one, carefully drawn and
washed in delicately, very unlike his earlier style.

129 EDWARD LEAR (1812–88)
Cedars of Lebanon [8¼ × 12⅛ ins.]: Inse.
Lear was above all a linear artist, and every line in this
example is significant. We must assume, as usual with his
work, that any necessary colour was added in the studio,
and indeed we can see the notes written on the spot for
guidance—'snow' on the left between the trunks of the
cedars, and 'green' in the space between their roots.

130 SAMUEL READ
(c. 1815–83)
Münster [10 × 13 ins.]

Samuel Read drew a series of haunted houses which were engraved for the *Illustrated London News*, and he was sent abroad to the Continent by that journal to cover the Crimean War. His water-colours are mainly continental street scenes and church interiors, the former very much in the style of Callow, and the latter very carefully drawn in pencil, washed in and heightened with body-colour which Read used for stained-glass windows, the subdued light in side-chapels and chancels, and the faces and tonsured heads of his monks

132 RICHARD DADD (1817–87)

The Passions: Idleness [14¾ × 10⅛ ins.]

Richard Dadd was born at Chatham and educated at the Royal
Academy Schools. About 1842 he travelled to Egypt, where he did
some fine landscapes. In 1843 he had a mental breakdown during
which he murdered his father. He was confined for the rest of his life
first at Bethlehem Hospital and later at Broadmoor. During his
imprisonment he constantly painted groups of the kind reproduced
here. The paintings have a feel for detail—almost Pre-Raphaelite—
but the faces all seem to reflect Dadd's own insanity.

131 JOHN ABSOLON (1815–95)

Cliffs by the Sea [9¼ × 15 ins.]

John Absolon was born at Lambeth. He was very talented and at
various times portrait painter, theatrical scene painter, topographical
artist, book illustrator and, especially, marine artist. He was closely
connected with the New Water-colour Society, being its treasurer
for some years. *Cliffs by the Sea* is a sparkling water-colour with
all the panache of Boudin and in style anticipating Wilson Steer.

133 JOHN RUSKIN
(1819–1900)
Zermatt

[$10\frac{3}{4} \times 15\frac{1}{16}$ ins.]: Inse.
John Ruskin was
as proficient and
as incisive with
his brush as he
was with his pen,
and drawings such
as this, which is
in pencil and wash,
were made during
his extensive
Continental travels. The
treatment of the
mountains is especially
fine, drawn with a
detail that, since
the eye looks
naturally up to the
peaks, would be
superfluous in the
foreground, and was
accordingly omitted.

238

134 HERCULES BRABAZON BRABAZON (1821–1906)

Ischia [$7\frac{5}{16} \times 11\frac{5}{8}$ ins.]: S.

Brabazon made tours in Spain, Egypt and India, among other places, and he studied at Rome for three years. His work invariably shows great awareness of impressions of nature, which he was able to record in harmonious colour. The pre-

liminary drawing in water-colours of this kind is apparently
haphazard, but when it is combined with glowing, scintil-
lating colour applied in a mosaic of splashes and blots,
which appeals to the senses rather than to the mind, the
planned result is the epitomy of the heat, the sunlight
and the dust of the Mediterranean coast.

135 FREDERICK GOODALL (1822–1904)

The Children of Charles I [12 × 17½ ins.]: S. and D. 1862

Goodall's reputation was built not only upon Eastern subjects which resulted from travel to Egypt but also upon pictures of historical incidents. The composition of this fine example 'hangs together' excellently; it is precisely drawn and fully detailed, for this kind of work, and this kind of rather sentimental, nostalgic subject was demanded by the public of Goodall's day.

136 MYLES BIRKET FOSTER [1825–99]

Children Playing [13¼ × 27⅝ ins.]

Birket Foster travelled on the Continent, and his drawings of scenes in Venice, on the Rhine and in Brittany, as well as of places in this country, are prized by collectors. He also drew for *Punch* and the *Illustrated London News*, and made lovely little vignettes, exquisitely drawn and daintily coloured, or merely pencilled, or to be made into engravings, to illustrate books of poetry or to be used on the fly-leaves of novels. Above all, however, he is best known for his beautifully stippled rustic landscapes, with children playing.

138 THOMAS BUSH HARDY
(1842–97)
Wreck off Holy Island
[12¾ × 21¼ ins.]: S. and D.

In his day Hardy's vividly coloured water-colours of stormy seas were very popular and he was highly regarded as a marine painter. The result of his popularity was that many of his drawings were stereotyped, and give the impression that they were 'pot-boilers'. On the other hand, not only was he capable of painting miniature drawings, full of meticulously penned detail and mostly done during his travels in Holland and Italy, but his coastal scenes can be equally well done, though in his usual apparently hasty style. The drawings done during the seventies and eighties, of which this is an example, are usually his best.

137 EDMUND MORISON WIMPERIS (1835–1900)

Windsor Castle [10 × 13⅞ ins.]: S.

A usual Wimperis style, with the sky about half the area of the drawing. It was probably completed out-of-doors, and in its directness and simplicity more pleasing than the kind of detailed work which Wimperis sometimes did in his studio. The foreground, owing much in its treatment not only to Collier but also to a lesser degree to Cox, is very typical and repays study. Wimperis had some training under Birket Foster and at first worked in the same painstaking way.

139 WALTER CRANE (1845–1915)

Olyn Elsie, near Bettws-y-Coed [15½ × 24½ ins.]: S. and D.

Walter Crane was born in Liverpool, and at the early age of fourteen
illustrated Tennyson's *Lady of Shalott*. Most of his early work
consisted of illustrations for children's books of great skill
and decorative quality. Stylistically he was much influenced by
the Pre-Raphaelites and William Morris. Crane also painted portraits,
landscapes and designs for tapestries and wall-papers.

140 ALBERT GOODWIN (1845–1932)

Canterbury [12$\frac{3}{8}$ × 19$\frac{1}{2}$ ins.]: S.

Goodwin shared with his fellow Pre-Raphaelite A. W. Hunt an intense admiration for Turner, though the stippling style he often used is reminiscent of the work of Birket Foster, however much more sophisticated. He was but fifteen when he

first exhibited at the Academy, and when in 1881 he was
elected a full member his work was almost wholly in water-
colour. This drawing, with the cathedral tower glimmering
mysteriously white against the darker sky and foliage, is
typically delicate, and shows Goodwin's penchant for misty
evening effects, and his clever use of elusive light.

141 KATE GREENAWAY (1846–1901)

An Illustration to 'A Day in a Child's Life' [7⅛ × 5 ins.]: S.

This drawing is typical of the genre painting of the later Victorian years, a suitable subject for an engraving of the kind beloved not only in the nurseries but also in the parlours of our grandparents, who insisted upon what to them was everyday realism.

142 PHILIP WILSON STEER (1860–1942)

Stroud, Gloucester [7½ × 9¾ ins.]

Steer was born at Birkenhead, and studied at the École des Beaux Arts in Paris. The result was that he resolved to develop a new freedom in painting, which led to the formation of the New English Art Club. In this example we see Steer's swift, unlaboured drawing which creates an impression rather than a detailed likeness, his dashing treatment of colour washes, and his effective use of hard edges to them. It must always be difficult to learn to recognise an artist's style from a photograph, since so many factors are eliminated, but this particular illustration is well worth close study in this regard.

143 ARTHUR RACKHAM (1867–1939)

Midsummer Night's Dream [13 × 8¼ ins.]: S. and D. 1909

Arthur Rackham studied art at the Lambeth School of Art and later at the Slade. Like Dulac and Greenaway, he was an instinctive illustrator with a natural gift for visually interpreting imaginative stories like *Grimm's Fairy Tales*, *Peter Pan* and such like books. His style was very detailed and Gothic but never objectionably macabre. Much of his illustration work was in full colour, but colour applied over a basic line drawing and very delicate in tone. Rackham's last, and perhaps best-known, work was the set of illustrations to Kenneth Grahame's *Wind in the Willows*. In addition to his illustrative work he was a talented landscape painter with a sensitive eye for light.

INDEX

(The bold figures refer to illustrations)